Religion and Wine

Religion and Wine

A Cultural History of Wine Drinking in the United States

Robert C. Fuller

The University of Tennessee Press • Knoxville

The paper used in this book meets the minimum requirements of ANSI/NISO
Z39.48-1992 (R 1997) (Permanence of Paper). The binding materials have
been chosen for strength and durability. Printed on recycled paper.

Library of Congress Cataloging-in-Publication Data

Fuller, Robert C., 1952–
    Religion and wine: a cultural history of wine drinking in the United States/
        Robert C. Fuller.—1st ed.
          p.   cm.
Includes bibliographical references and index.
ISBN 0-87049-910-6 (cloth: alk paper)
ISBN 0-87049-911-4 (pbk: alk paper)
1. Wine and wine making—United States—History.
2. Wine and wine making—Religious aspects.
3. Temperance and religion—United States.
I. Title
TP557.F85   1996
394.1'3—dc20   95-4379
                                     CIP

Contents

Illustrations

Foreword

It was Christmas in New York, 1948. That autumn, I had joined the faculty of Union Theological Seminary in my first appointment after completing my doctorate at the University of Chicago. In addition to my own teaching responsibilities, I was assigned as an assistant to the world-renowned theologian, Paul Tillich. The first German professor to be personally dismissed on order of Hitler, Tillich fled with his family to the United States. His fame spread until, in the 1950s, his picture graced the cover of *Time*. When the magazine celebrated its fortieth anniversary in 1963, Henry Luce invited all living celebrities who'd been on the cover to attend a several-days' gala celebration. The two major speakers for the great banquet were to be President John F. Kennedy—who had to decline at the last moment, so Secretary of State Dean Rusk substituted—and Professor Paul Tillich. Such was his fame.

As a Christmas gift, Tillich presented the Brauers with two bottles of fine German wine, a Mosel and a Rhinegau, and requested that when they were ready to drink the wine they should call him so he could come over and explain the wine. He informed me that it should be prepared at 52 to 55 degrees, and that we must use proper German wine glasses. We had a late 1930s refrigerator in our Union Seminary apartment that, at best, was unreliable as to temperature. Also, we had no German wine glasses. We purchased the proper glasses and a thermometer for the refrigerator thinking the entire affair to be somewhat foolish; nevertheless, we looked forward to the occasion.

After making our preparations one day, we called Tillich to come over that evening and initiate us into the mysteries of German wine, or better yet into the mysteries of wine. Muriel and I knew virtually nothing about wine. Though I preferred wine to beer, in spite of my name and heritage, the American wines that I drank from time to time were not very good. Even a neophyte recognized that much. Tillich arrived, inspected the glasses, declared them acceptable, checked the temperatures of the bottles, gave his approval, sat down, and asked us to join him so we could properly enjoy the wine. In a very heavy German accent he proceeded to enlighten us.

"First," said Tillich, "it is necessary to understand what wine really is. Truly, it is the nectar of the gods. There is no other drink like it known to humanity. Only wine is used in religions as a sacramental drink. In fact, wine is like the incarnation—it is both divine and human." Muriel and I exchanged glances of curiosity as to what Tillich was about. He appeared serious, yet there was a twinkle in his eye and a slight smile on his lips.

Continuing his discourse, Tillich said, "Wine is divine, a gift of God. Where did the vines come from? From God—we did not make them. But the vines need a very special soil. That is the gift of the gods. Also, the soil must lay just right—in some places steep, in others flat. That is the gift of the gods. And, there must be just the right amount of rain at just the proper time—not too much, not too little, not too early, not too late. That is a divine gift. Above all, the sunshine—again, not too cold, not too hot, all at just the right time. This too is a gift of the divine."

At this point, Muriel and I were on the edge of our chairs. Tillich continued, "Wine is both divine and human. The vines and grapes are from the gods. But only humans learn which grapes to use—through human knowledge alone—and improve the stock; humans carefully tend the vines, learn when to pick the grapes—all this is human. It is human experience that prepares the grapes to become wine—they stomp out the juice with their feet, they prepare the juice to ferment, but the fermenting itself is divine. Humans place wine in barrels that humans make of just the right wood, and at just the right time put it in bottles they make." At this point, Tillich had convinced the young Brauers that, indeed, wine was both divine and human, but he was not finished. He went on to say, "Now you see that wine is special. Only wine of all drinks continues to live and grow in the bottle. First, it is a baby, then it is a child, then it enters puberty and becomes a teenager, then it becomes a young adult, then wine reaches its full maturity, and slowly it enters old age—some wines gracefully, some harshly, and then it dies. Of all drinks, wine alone recapitulates life. This is why wine is a sacrament."

Tillich continued. He asked that we now bring out the glasses and the wine. He carefully felt the bottles and declared the wine ready. He pointed out to us that Mosel is always in a green bottle of a certain shape and that Rhine is in a brown bottle of a similar shape. He indicated that this was an easy way to spot which wine one was drinking if one was not an expert. He reached into his pocket and pulled out a large Swiss army knife that looked like a miniature tool chest. He flipped open a good-size corkscrew and demonstrated how, in the absence of more so-phisticated instruments, one places the bottle between one's knees and pulls the cork. He pointed out that one sniffs the cork for the scent of vinegar, but that is unnecessary for a young wine.

He carefully took the glass by the stem, poured in a small amount of wine, held it to the light, swirled the wine gently for a few moments, put his nose in the glass and inhaled several times, then he took a mouthful and swished it for several moments, drank it and pronounced it excellent. All this time, puzzled, we watched the ritual, each step of which was later explained to us, then he poured our wine and invited us to drink. When we picked up our glasses, he quickly told us to hold the glasses only by the stem, or the glasses would not ring properly when touched together in toasting, and there would be smudges on the clear crystal. Also, the hand can pass heat to the bowl when held in the hand. He pointed out that there was no mystery to any of this; it was simply common sense. Finally, we touched our glasses in a toast and imbibed what, indeed, had become for us a gift of the gods, truly divine and truly human. We were launched on a lifetime of exploration of the mys-teries and sheer pleasure of wine.

At last we have a book that explores the interrelationship between religion and wine in the United States. It is not the first book on reli-gion and wine, it is not the first book on wine in the United States, but it is the first and only book on religion and wine in the United States. As such, it deserves a careful reading by historians, particularly cultural, re-ligious, and social historians, by anthropologists, by sociologists, and by theologians. Further, it will be of special interest to enologists and to those who love wine. It is one of those rare books that appeals to and is neces-sary for the experts, yet also appeals to and will delight a substantial portion of our population—those who appreciate and are knowledge-able about wine. There is something unique about the way religion and wine have interacted in the culture of the United States. No other west-ern nation undertook an effort to ban by law the manufacture, distribu-tion, and sale of all alcoholic beverages. This fact alone poses a funda-mental question—why did it occur? Fuller does a masterful job of analyzing the interrelationship between wine and religion in America that explains the phenomenon of prohibition in our culture.

Prohibition is only one side of the question. As Fuller demonstrates, religion was responsible for introducing and sustaining viniculture in the United States, and wine was integral to the religious practice and drinking habits of the vast majority of religious people in America until the nineteenth century. These are the interrelationships that intrigue historians, anthropologists, and sociologists. There are no simple answers, but Fuller establishes that there are answers. They find their sources in the interplay between a wide variety of dimensions of life within the United States—ethnic, demographic, geographical, religious, psychological, and sociological.

Perhaps the most intriguing point of Robert Fuller's study is his exploration of the development of a post-Prohibition wine culture in America. His perceptive linking of the rise of that culture to the emergence of new forms of popular religion in America is a fresh insight that should provoke considerable discussion. The timing of the book could not be better. At the moment when there is a renewed effort— perhaps a neo-prohibitionist effort—to link wine with drug addiction, this book will compel all thoughtful people to gain a fresh perspective on wine in the culture of the United States—past, present, and future.

Jerald C. Brauer
Naomi Shenstone Donnelley Professor Emeritus
and the Frederick W. Bateson Senior Professor in Residence

Acknowledgments

Many thanks need to be offered for the assistance I have received while researching this book. First and foremost, I would like to thank Debbie Doering for printing and formatting countless drafts of this manuscript. I would also like to thank Duane Zehr for processing many of the photos appearing in this book. And, too, Marina Savoie and her staff in the Interlibrary Loan Department of Bradley University's library deserve recognition for helping me gain access to the materials needed to finish the research for this book.

Among those who provided assistance to me in acquiring research materials were James L. Kimball Jr., archivist for the Church of Jesus Christ of Latter-day Saints; Ron Numbers of the University of Wisconsin; and Linda Walker Stevens of Hermann, Missouri. I would also like to acknowledge the *Journal of American Culture* for granting me permission to reprint portions of an article entitled "Religion and Ritual in American Wine Culture" that appeared in the spring 1993 issue. The photo credits acknowledge those individuals and institutions that provided me with illustrations for this manuscript; their assistance was invaluable and greatly appreciated.

A special thanks to my enological colleagues Steve Preece, Leo Wine, Tom Farmer, Roger Otterstrom, Margaret Farmer, and Kathy Fuller. They have taught me much about the aesthetics of wine.

Finally, I would like to acknowledge the great debt I owe to Jerald Brauer, Naomi Shenstone Donnelley Professor of American Religious History Emeritus and former Dean of the Divinity School of the University of Chicago. My former mentor and dissertation adviser, Dr. Brauer taught me both the art and skill of studying American religious life. But perhaps even more importantly, Jerry also passed on his enthusiasm for the appreciation of wine. The adeptness of Jerry Brauer's palate is matched only by the personal and professional generosity he offered his students over many decades. The inspiration for this book came during lengthy conversations in his legendary cellar, and I would consequently like to dedicate this book to him in honor of his unparalleled gift for teaching graduate students.

Introduction

The story of wine in America has been told from many perspectives.[1] Some versions have focused upon the role that economic and commercial factors have played in shaping the American wine industry. Others have highlighted the way in which geographical variables, such as climate or soil composition, have determined the course of the wine industry. Still others have related the history of America's wines to advances in scientific agriculture and wine-production technology. Yet no one has seriously explored the development of wine in the United States in relationship to American religion. This is somewhat surprising owing to the obvious ways in which religion and wine are intermingled in our common experience. For example, Catholics, Episcopalians, and Lutherans collectively make up almost one-third of the American population. How curious it must be to them that their worship is not considered valid without wine. In sharp contrast are the Baptists, Methodists, and various holiness churches, such as the Assemblies of God or the Church of the Nazarene, who have historically assumed that the use of wine for worship will incur the wrath, not the gracious pleasure, of their Lord. Why is it that Jews do not consider either marriages or Sabbath services complete without the ritual presence of wine? And why is it that of all alcoholic beverages, wine is the drink we associate with the christening of ships, romantic dinners and conversations, or the celebration of great accomplishments?

What follows is a cultural history of the influence that religion has had upon the production and consumption of wine in the United States. The word culture here refers to the prevailing attitudes, dispositions, and lifestyles that both characterize and provide structure to everyday life in the United States. Culture includes the dominant moral and aesthetic styles, the general world view, and prevailing attitudes concerning the "good life." Religion, particularly Protestantism, has had a pervasive influence upon American culture and for this reason has also had particular effects upon Americans' understandings of the significance of wine drinking. This historical survey will, for example, chronicle the great extent to which viniculture in the United States was started and sustained by religious groups. It will also reveal important interconnections between religion and wine in American cultural life. For example, wine—like religion—has had its own influence upon American culture insofar as it, too, shapes people's aesthetic styles and attitudes concerning the "good life." In the view of many people who participate in our culture, both wine and religion uplift people's spirits and engender the conviction that they enrich our lives or, at the very least, make them more endurable. The consumption of wine, as with participation in religious rituals, makes it possible for individuals to experience or release certain emotions that are deemed incommensurate with everyday behavior. And, importantly, both tend to elicit from us a certain "aesthetic" sensibility; that is, they deepen our sense of relatedness to the world and evoke experiences that blur the distinction between ourselves (the subject) and what we are experiencing (the object). These parallels between the ways in which religion and wine function in our cultural life make the story of their historical interaction fascinating; they also help alert us to the reasons why there has always been a special relationship between wine and humanity's spiritual or religious nature. While much has been written about the "deification" of wine in ancient Egypt, Greece, or Rome, it is also important that we have some historical sense of the interaction of religion and wine in the American context.

Religion and Wine through History

The cultural connection between religion and the experience of wine drinking is hardly unique to the United States. There is, perhaps, no cultural tradition that goes back further in recorded history. The use of wine probably started well before 4241 B.C.E., the year that the Egyptians began marking time with a calendar.[2] The ancient world's practice of storing grapes in earthen jars caused accidental fermentation to occur with changes in moisture and temperature. Although the bubbling juice might have been thrown away at first, it did not take long to discover its intoxicating effects. Of course, the ancient world knew of other intoxicating substances, too. Poppy juice, hallucinogenic mushrooms, peyote, and the leaves of the coca plant have all been associated with religious ecstasy. As Edward Hyams has written, "[T]he strange

Vineyard scene in Egyptian tomb painting from the time of Ramesses II. Courtesy of The Metropolitan Museum of Art.

power of intoxicants to release the human spirit from the control of mind led to their being regarded with superstitious awe and, seized upon by shamans, witchdoctors and priests, they became early and everywhere instruments of religious experience. Their use became a religious rite, and this was the case of wine as of the others."[3] Over the long haul of world history, wine has proven to be religion's stimulant of choice. One reason for this is surely that wine is less deleterious and liable to dangerous abuse than the other benign poisons we use to justify God's ways.[4] Grape vines are also more adaptable than most other intoxicating plants. The yield per acre and per man hour from viticulture has traditionally been higher than almost any other form of agriculture. Yet, whatever the precise mixture of reasons, wine established itself in the ancient world as the beverage of the gods and was almost always associated with religious feasts and libations offered to please the deities who control our fate.

Wine was vital to the ancient world's celebration of life. One wine vase identified as belonging to an Egyptian royal family, for example, bears an inscription extolling the vase's contents as fit for the gods themselves. The Egyptians apparently believed that wine was to be enjoyed in the afterlife as well. Many ancient tombs depict wine jars being offered to the dead; in some cases, whole vineyards are decorously painted on a tomb's walls and ceiling. Egyptian religion associated certain divinities with this blessed gift of nature. Both Osiris and Hathor were variously identified as the patron gods of wine. Hathor, who was represented as a sacred cow, was duly honored on a monthly "Day of Intoxication."

Several ancient religions developed mythical accounts of the creation of wine from the body of a primordial divine being.[5] For example, an Iranian legend recounts how wine originated from the blood of the ritual sacrifice of a primordial bull. Each year's crushing of grapes thereby reenacts this sacrificial slaughter and the resulting wine is consequently thought capable of bestowing the bull's strength, energy, and vital force upon those who consume it. This motif of the creation of an intoxicant from the body of a primordial divine being has its parallels in many other religions, not the least of which is Christianity's belief that one who drinks sacramental wine takes Christ's essential nature and his very blood within his or her own body.[6]

Ancient Greek civilization similarly honored its wines by connecting them with the gods they depicted in their mythology. Not blessed with fertile soil that would have permitted the cultivation of numerous varieties of foods, the rocky soil and numerous hillsides of Greece at least favored the growing of grapes. Wine, along with olive oil, provided the ancient Greeks with a precious export commodity that they could use to trade in the Mediterranean world. Wine also became the focal point of Greek social life and was lavishly praised by Greek poets as the veritable fountain of civilized life and thought. The god Dionysos was hailed as the giver of all good gifts and was attributed with being the patron of wine. Dionysos was said to offer ecstasy, spiritual vision, and wild intoxication to his devotees. As one historian notes, "The Dionysian worshipper at the height of his ecstasy was one with his god. Divinity had entered into him."[7] Such was the religious imagination of a people who found in wine a vehicle to the highest enjoyment of philosophy and poetry.

The Romans in large part adopted the religious pantheon of Greek mythology. Yet, at least originally, it was not Dionysos (or Bacchus in the Roman version) who was identified with wine but none other than Jupiter himself. Jupiter, the great god of the air, light, and heat, was also accredited with having bestowed upon humanity the gift of wine. In ancient Rome, as in Greece, most of the festivals that emerged as spontaneous expressions of human celebration coincided with the most important phases of the grape-growing and wine-producing agricultural cycle.

Although our direct concern is with those religious traditions that

Bronze sculpture of Bacchus, god of wine, by Louis Granier (c. 1638–1728). Courtesy of The Metropolitan Museum of Art.

have in some way influenced American popular culture, it is interesting to note that wine is closely connected with religious attitudes in Asia as well. In contemporary Japan, for example, rice wine (sake) is commonly placed on the family altar. Wine is intimately associated with rituals and ceremonies honoring the *kami*, or divine beings. For this reason there are large casks of sake located at almost all of the major Shinto shrines. Because of wine's association with the *kami*, it is also present in Japanese wedding ceremonies for the toasts that the bride and groom make to one another and is also used in such ceremonies as the dedication of a new home or building.

Throughout Chinese history wine has been intimately associated with religious offerings. Even today, wine is placed on altars in businesses or restaurants in honor of the god of prosperity or other protective deities. On Chinese New Year and other holidays, wine is offered to ancestors as a token of the indissoluble union of family ties. On the holiday known as the "Spring Sweeping of the Graves," wine is brought

Wine offered to protective deities on a Chinese altar. Photo by Duane Zehr.

to the ancestral burial grounds and first offered to the spirits before being consumed by the living. Wine is not, however, found in specifically
Buddhist ceremonies in either China or Japan since Buddhist monks
take a vow to refrain from the use of all intoxicants.

There is a similar absence of wine in the world's second-largest religion, Islam, owing to the Muslim prohibition of alcoholic beverages.
The prohibition of wine was apparently not one of Muhammad's original concerns.[8] The Quran positively associates wine with the grace of
God. One verse, for example, even praises wine as one of the signs of
Allah's grace unto humanity: "And of the fruit of palm trees, and of
grapes, ye obtain an inebriating liquor, and also good nourishment."
Another verse lists bountiful supplies of wine as one of the pleasures
that the faithful might look forward to after final judgment. Describing
the garden that the righteous are promised, the Quran states that "in it are
rivers of water incorruptible; rivers of milk of which the taste never changes;
rivers of wine, a joy to those who drink; and rivers of honey pure and
clear." Apparently, however, Muhammad was sufficiently outraged
by the drunken excesses of his followers to condemn the drinking of

wine. For example, commentaries on the Quran relate how Muhammad's companions held drinking parties that led to their failure to observe ritual prayer. Tradition also has it that Muhammad's uncle, Hamza b. 'Abd al-Muttalib, mutilated his son Ali's camels in a fit of drunkenness. Other followers evidently took not only to excessive wine drinking but also to gambling, which eventually prompted Muhammad's condemnation of these vices. A verse from the Quran made this prohibition explicit: "O true believers! Surely wine and gambling and stone pillars and divining arrows are an abomination, of the work of Satan; therefore avoid them, that ye may prosper."

The biblical culture of ancient Judaism was, with the exception of its attitudes toward drunkenness, much more positive about the joys and spiritual meanings of wine drinking. Wine was not a luxury in ancient Mediterranean culture; it was a staple of every life, drunk by all classes and all ages. The Bible attributes Noah with the first cultivation of grapes and the making of wine. After the Flood had receded and the inhabitants of the Ark had disembarked, Noah became "the first tiller of the soil. He planted a vineyard; and he drank of the wine, and became drunk" (Gen. 9:20). Throughout the Old Testament, wine is depicted as a sign of God's blessing (Gen. 27:28; Deut. 7:13; Amos 9:14). An extraordinary abundance of wine was interpreted as a harbinger of the Messianic Age (Amos 9:13, Joel 3:18; Zech. 9:17). Importantly, what most commended wine to the writers of the Old Testament was its ability to alter moods and to raise a person's spirits. The "gladdening of the heart" that wine created was not only thought to be acceptable, but was positively recommended (2 Sam. 13:28; Esther 1:10; Ps. 104:15; Eccl. 9:7 and 10:19; Zech. 9:15 and 10:7).

Wine continued to be a part of both religious and family celebrations in Jewish culture through the New Testament period. This is clearly indicated, for example, in the account of the wedding at Cana where Jesus is attributed with his first public miracle: the turning of water into wine so that it might be available for the celebration of life. The fact that the early Christian community continued to embrace wine as an essential part of life is indicated by Paul's advice to his reader to "take a little wine for your stomach's sake" (1 Tim. 5:23). Paul's counsel, especially when combined with scriptural passages that refer to the power of wine to "gladden the heart," makes it clear that the Bible was extolling the spiritual merits of wine, not of unfermented grape juice, despite the claims of some ultraconservative Bible students who, as early as the nineteenth-century temperance movements, began earnest efforts to disassociate wine from biblical religion.

Not only did wine drinking continue as an essential part of the cultures spawned by Judaism and Christianity, it also became a central part of their religious ceremonies. The Seder meal in Judaism and the Christian sacrament of communion both illustrate how fully the subtle pleasures of wine drinking became associated with the religious urge both to find union with God and friendship with one another. It is important to note that throughout the Middle Ages, the Church was the repository of the skills of civilization that would otherwise have been lost following the fall of Rome. Reading, writing, and wine making were preserved in Western Civilization for hundreds of years by the Roman Catholic clergy. Hugh Johnson has noted, "As expansionist monasteries cleared hillsides and walled round fields of cuttings, as dying winegrowers bequeathed it their land, the Church came to be identified with wine—not only as the Blood of Christ, but as luxury and comfort in this world."[9] For well over a thousand years almost all the best vineyards of Europe were owned and cultivated by Roman Catholic monks.[10] And, too, monks presided over every stage of the wine-making process and perfected many of the fermentation and bottling techniques still used today. The most famous of all monk vignerons is undoubtedly the Frenchman Dom Perignon who, somewhat by accident, discovered how wine could be made to go through a second fermentation and yield sparkling wines such as those that have made his home district of Champagne famous. It is told that upon his first sip of this elegant wine, Dom Perignon proclaimed "I drink stars." This triumphant exclamation is, perhaps, purely apocryphal, but the legend of Dom Perignon's skills as a cellarmaster reminds us of how fully the Christian tradition has promoted the production of quality wines both for the celebration of Mass and for the celebration of daily living.

Wine and American Culture

It is within this larger historical context that our story of the cultural interaction between religion and wine in America reveals its full significance. The creativity of the New World can be seen in the ways in which it borrowed from and elaborated upon its European heritage. The story of this "creative borrowing" will contribute to our understanding of at least two aspects of American popular life and culture. First, it will make an original contribution to our understanding of the development of "wine culture" in this country by identifying the ways in which religion has shaped Americans' attitudes concerning the influence wine has upon their health, psychological well-being, and moral character. This study will consequently have relevance to the sociological and anthropological study of alcohol use. While the social scientific study of alcohol consumption has typically focused on the etiology of pathological drinking, there is an increasing interest in the larger social and cultural contexts that influence the ways in which people consume alcohol.[11] The history of American wine drinking potentially responds to Claude Levi-Strauss's invitation to "discover how, in any particular case, [dietary practices are] a language through which that society unconsciously translates its structure."[12] Americans' attitudes and patterns of consuming wine—as well as their taboos forbidding its use—can be seen to be intimately connected with the "structure" of ideas and sentiments generated by their religious heritage.

Secondly, the diversity of ways in which religion and wine have interacted over the course of American cultural history opens up new perspectives on the nation's religious imagination. Wine, for example, has been central to the rituals of communal affirmation in most American religious groups, particularly those with strong communitarian commitments. Wine has also played an important part in ritualizing several religious movements' concern with cultivating emotional and intellectual spontaneity. Interest in theological innovation, it seems, has frequently been fostered by the expansive emotions associated with wine drinking. And as we shall see in the fifth chapter, this is particularly true in the emergence in recent decades of a form of "popular religion" centered in the aesthetics of wine drinking. The concluding section of this book will attempt to draw final attention to a variety of roles that wine has performed in the American context: promoting communal bonding, fostering celebratory social interaction, affording individuals the felt sense of directly communing with divinity, and emboldening persons to strike out in novel theological directions. Indeed, scholars have devoted considerable attention to the ways that an intoxicating beverage such as soma affected the religious though of ancient India or how the ritual drinking of yage influences South American religion. Yet, no one has as yet given sustained attention to the role of wine in the American religious context. A final contribution of this historical narrative will, then, be the insight it offers concerning the role that the "nectar of the gods" has had in shaping the spiritual experience of persons both inside and outside the nation's established religious institutions.

CHAPTER 1

Religion, Wine, and Eastern "High Culture"

Our history books are fond of narrating a story about the settlement of North America by Europeans seeking some combination of religious freedom and commercial opportunity. Historical evidence hardly justifies adding the pursuit of vinicultural happiness to the list of principal motives for the settlement of North America. Nonetheless, the promise of the pleasures to be extracted from American wines surely gave additional incentive to those willing to brave the sparse New World in pursuit of either worldly or heavenly riches. During the early eleventh century, for example, Leif Ericsson is said to have sailed his Viking ship along the eastern coast of North America where he saw such a bounty of wild grapes growing that he called the New World "Vinland."[1] About five hundred years later, in 1562, the French Huguenots came to Florida in search of freedom to pursue their Protestant faith and immediately began producing wine from the native Scuppernong grapes. Subsequent waves of Huguenot settlements brought wine-making expertise to the fledgling colonies in Rhode Island, Virginia, Massachusetts, and Pennsylvania. Similarly, the first permanent English settlement in Jamestown, established in 1607, was already growing grapes by 1609.[2] Even the Pilgrims set themselves to making wine shortly after they landed at Plymouth, and it is possible that they already had wine to celebrate the first Thanksgiving in 1623.[3]

From the outset, then, wine had much to do with sustaining the strong spirit with which the early colonists settled the new frontiers of American civilization. Both agnostic entrepreneurs and believers of various religious traditions viewed wine as a reminder of the finer things they nostalgically associated with European culture. Insofar as wine symbolized the enjoyment of culture's higher accomplishments, it was a commodity prized by the educated leaders of the colonial era. Settlers along the East Coast struggled valiantly, but for the most part in vain, to produce this same civilizing influence in the New World.

Seventeenth-Century Beginnings

Although William Bradford wrote in his diary that the Pilgrims saw "vines everywhere" when they landed at Plymouth Bay in 1621, there is no solid evidence to indicate just when they set themselves to the task of producing wine. We do know, however, that the nearby Massachusetts Bay Colony began making wine from native grapes within weeks of their arrival. The colony's governor, John Winthrop, exhorted his fellow settlers to construct a community based entirely upon faithful obedience to God. He fervently believed that God intended the settlers in America to create "a city set on a hill" from which "the eyes of the world" would learn the glory of a civil government patterned solely upon the dictates of God. Hand in hand with Winthrop's lofty theocratic vision was his eagerness to see wine flowing plentifully from this city on a hill. He thus acquired Governor's Island in Boston Harbor for the purpose of planting vineyards and was among the earliest colonial leaders to experience the futility of trying to grow European grapes in America.

The early colonial period was dominated by Protestants and, more specifically, by those Protestants whose beliefs fell under the heading of "Puritan." The term Puritan refers to those Protestants who adhered to the basic tenets of John Calvin's stern theology and who consequently emphasized the importance of a personal conversion experience wherein an individual received assurance of his or her salvation. Although Puritans in the colonial period were strict with regard to theology, they enjoyed the blessings that God bestowed upon creation far more than most modern Americans assume. Not least among these blessings was alcohol. As Emil Oberholzer observes in his study of Puritan Congregationalism in early Massachusetts, "The 'Puritan' who shuddered at the very sight (or thought) of a glass of beer or wine, not to mention hard liquor, did not live in colonial Massachusetts."[4] "Grape juice Protestants" became a phenomenon only in the nineteenth century (for reasons that will be discussed in chapter 4). Indeed, Puritans embraced the mood-elevating properties of alcohol as one aspect of natural happiness. The famed Congregationalist preacher, Rev. Increase Mather, called drink "a good creature of God."[5]

Mather fully embraced the enjoyment of God's bounteous gifts, as did other religious leaders in late-seventeenth-century New England, provided only that citizens not overindulge in this goodly creature. Hence, Mather not only extolled the God-given pleasures of wine, but was also quick to append the admonition that a person must not "drink a Cup of Wine more than is good for him."[6]

Protestants of the Puritan persuasion were not alone in coming to the New World for the expression of religious freedom and, once here, finding their new home hospitable to the enjoyment of a goodly cup of wine. The Quaker William Penn believed that America provided him the providential opportunity to found a "holy experiment." Penn yearned to create a society based squarely on the Christian gospel in which the practice of love and virtue would be "an example . . . to the nations." To help create his city of brotherly love, Penn brought French and Spanish vines to Philadelphia in 1683. He also drank a "good claret" made by a French Huguenot named Gabriel Rappel and began questioning whether the future of American wine making might actually lie not with the European vinifera varietals but rather with domestic vines. Debating the pros and cons of cultivating the native grapes as opposed to importing more European vines, he wrote, "[I]t seems most reasonable to believe, that not only a thing groweth best, where it naturally grows; but will hardly be equalled by another species of the same kind, that doth not naturally grow there. But to solve the doubt, I intend, if God give me life, to try both, and hope the consequence will be as good wine as any European countries of the same latitude do yield."[7] Unfortunately, Penn never pursued this plan to cultivate the domestic varietals. Opting instead to work with the European vinifera rootstock, his viticultural efforts never proved successful.

Maryland's Lord Baltimore, whose name comes down to us as synonymous with Roman Catholics' pursuit of religious freedom, also tried growing grapes for the purpose of producing wine. As early as 1662, Lord Baltimore planted some three hundred acres of vines and was able to sell large quantities of wines that were reputed to compare favorably with those of the Burgundy district in France.[8] A decade later Lord Baltimore sent over more vines to his son, Charles Calvert, who had been appointed governor of the colony. Within a year the entire vineyard had gone to ruin, again thwarting the effort to grow European varietals in the New World.

As mentioned earlier, a good deal of the early viticulture (i.e., the cultivation of grapes) and viniculture (i.e., the production of wine) in the colonies built upon the skills of the Huguenot settlements. The Huguenots were French Protestants who were forced to flee their predominantly Catholic homeland owing to intense religious persecution. A good many fled to the Netherlands and England and, from there, to various colonial settlements that promised religious freedom. Those who ventured to North America were struck by its wild vines and prom-

ising terrain. The Huguenots were among the first to recognize the pos-
sibilities of native vines and learned to cultivate them to make drinkable, sometimes excellent wines.[9] The Huguenots' viticultural skills
stimulated the early wine industries in colonies ranging up and down
the Atlantic coast, including Florida, South Carolina, Virginia, Rhode
Island, and Pennsylvania.

A number of German Protestant groups also contributed to the beginnings of a wine industry in the seventeenth-century colonies. A
group of German Pietists settled in Germantown, Pennsylvania, in
1683, for example, and planned from the outset to specialize in wine
making. The settlement's leader, Francis Pastorius, wrote that they were
"especially anxious to advance the cultivation of the vine."[10] A few decades
later Protestant refugees from the Rhenish Palatinate (Rheinpfalz) region
of Germany also began settling in the American colonies and brought with
them a great deal of wine-making knowledge and a heritage rich in the
appreciation of wine drinking. As the next chapter makes clear, other
settlements by German religious groups, such as the Rappites and Amana
colonies, later contributed significantly to the spread of wine production across North America.

Wine and Countervailing Religious Attitudes

Despite the presence and even endorsement of wine among early
America's dominant religious groups, most of the early promotion of
"wine culture" in America came from those whose religious persuasion
went against the tide of the theological outlook promulgated by the
country's churches. From the outset, wine was associated with the upper social classes and, as a consequence, was most prevalent among
those whose religious beliefs were heavily influenced by either the deis-
tic or agnostic beliefs spawned by the Enlightenment. The reason for
this association between wine and the relatively small upper class was
partly economic and partly psychological. Economically, wine was an
expensive imported item that the lower and middle classes viewed as a
luxury they had to do without. Ralph Waldo Emerson, the great Transcendentalist philosopher whose book *Nature* (1832) has inspired successive generations of Americans to look within themselves for a point
of harmony with a universal spirit, wrote "I think wealth has lost much
of its value if it has not wine. I abstain from wine only on account of
the expense. When I heard that Mr. Sturgis had given up wine, I had
the same regret that I had lately in hearing that Mr. Bowditch had bro-
ken his hip."[11] In point of fact, Emerson was fairly well-to-do and be-

Lady pouring wine for a gentleman in early America. Originally published in J. E. Stebbins, *Fifty Years History of the Temperance Cause* (1874).

longed to New England's privileged upper class. But his association of wealth as a precondition of appreciating wine accurately characterizes the experience of most Americans until the expansion of commercial viniculture in California during the 1840s and 1850s.

The cheapest and thus most popular alcoholic beverage during the colonial period was rum, either imported from the British Indies or produced domestically from imported molasses. As domestic corn production increased and patriotic sentiments grew, whiskey gradually supplanted rum as the preferred "good creature of God" for Americans. In regions where orchards were plentiful, cider was also a popular beverage for the middle classes. By way of contrast, there was really no domestic supply of drinkable table wines. The vineyards planted by individuals such as Baltimore, Winthrop, or Penn quickly fell into ruin. The imported vines had root stock that was especially vulnerable to the cold

North American winters and to mildew, black rot, and a plant lice then unknown in Europe—phylloxera. Phylloxera was probably the most devastating. Farmers had no means to detect the presence and destructive effect of these tiny lice, let alone any experience with exterminating them. Not knowing the reason for their ruined vines, would-be American viniculturists experienced failure after failure in their efforts to grow successfully the grapes that produced the most prestigious European wines.

The native vines were not in the same vinifera family of vines found in Europe, but were instead of other species such as *labrusca*. Hearty and resistant to the as yet undetected phylloxera, the native species of vines unfortunately produced grapes whose flavors lacked the same kinds of subtle flavors associated with the best French, German, and Italian wines. As a consequence, most of the wine consumed by Americans during the colonial period was imported. The major wines of this period were from France or the Portuguese-occupied island of Madeira. The cost of the imported wine simply placed it beyond the pocketbook of most middle-class Americans. Thus, although the total gallons of wine consumed in America on a per capita basis today is roughly equal to the total gallons of distilled spirits, in the 1700s twenty times more spirits and cider were consumed than wine.[12]

In addition to the economic factors that fostered an association of wine with the upper class, there were other cultural and intellectual needs that prompted eastern "high society" to cherish their imported wines. W. J. Rorabaugh's perceptive study of alcohol consumption in the United States during the eighteenth and nineteenth centuries supports the contention that those Americans who drank wine had different psychological or emotional temperaments than their counterparts who preferred distilled liquor. He writes that "although whiskey and rum were cheaper and more readily available than beer or wine, it can be argued that these stronger beverages were selected for psychological rather than economic reasons."[13] Rorabaugh observes that if Americans had wanted to drink fermented beverages, most could have afforded them. Americans preferred distilled liquor not because it was so much cheaper, but because it was stronger. Throughout the colonial period and continuing into the first several decades of the early republic, the American middle class was simultaneously fueled by high aspirations, yet plagued by little inherited confidence that they could actually achieve all they aspired to. Rorabaugh, citing a host of social scientific studies on persons' motivations for consuming alcohol, contends that Americans turned to distilled spirits to help allay anxiety and produce feelings of inner power. He concludes:

If Horton's theory that drinking allays anxiety is correct, then we would expect the most potent alcoholic beverages to be used to cope with the greatest anxieties. And even though the strongest distilled beverages such as whiskey or rum are often drunk in diluted form, these diluted drinks usually contain more alcohol than nonspiritous beverages such as wine or beer. Thus, a person's choice of alcoholic beverage can be related to the level of his anxieties and, by inference, to the level of motivation for achievement and the level of aspirations.[14]

Rorabaugh's observations are undoubtedly sound as far as they go. But much more needs to be said about those whose material aspirations were largely met, and whose self-confidence or motivation was high rather than low. It may well be true that the middle and lower economic classes drank alcohol primarily to reduce internally generated sensations or tensions. Yet it might also be argued that the affluent and/or higher socioeconomic groups of Americans chose wine as their preferred beverage in disproportionately large numbers not to reduce internal excitation, but to enhance it. That is, there are always individuals who are motivated more to increase than to reduce intrapsychic sensations. Those persons who are less dominated by the need to enhance their economic or social status are frequently motivated to seek out activities that provide novelty or actually elicit mental exertion. It was among these, the affluent and culturally sophisticated, that wine was more psychologically appealing. Enjoying wine requires a great deal of accumulated knowledge concerning the unique characteristics of different grape varietals, the quality of distinct vintages, the role of proper cellaring, etc. Wine drinking thus provided upper-class gentlemen with an activity that was both aesthetically and intellectually stimulating. When they joined together in social settings to savor the subtle pleasures of a newly acquired bottle of imported wine they were simultaneously afforded the opportunity to engage in spirited discussion. In this sense wine rivaled religion as a vehicle for sublimating sensory pleasures into mental and spiritual activities for many of early America's upper-class citizenry.

The period encompassing the American Revolution witnessed the flowering of the philosophical movement known as the Enlightenment. This was an age in which educated persons gained newfound faith in human reason. Many of the movement's most influential spokesmen were led by their rational convictions to become indifferent or even hostile to institutional religion. During this age of reason, educated individuals tended to view the Bible as an ancient story book, full of crass supernaturalism and irrational beliefs. Enlightenment attitudes inspired the American colonial leaders with faith in human nature and the capacity of every individual to pursue the good life without unnecessary impositions from absolutist institutions. This anti-theological faith in human reason infected a high percentage of America's founding fathers. Typical of these were Benjamin Franklin and Thomas Jefferson. Franklin's wit was matched only by his love for wine. For the author of *Poor Richard's Almanac*, the religion of reason might well embrace wine as a kind of theological conduit through which God's wisdom is revealed to us. He mused,

> *In vino veritas*, say the wise men,—*Truth is in wine*. Before the days of Noah, then, men, having nothing but water to drink, could not discover the truth. Thus they went astray, became abominably wicked, and were justly exterminated by water, which they loved to drink. The good man Noah, seeing that through this pernicious beverage all his contemporaries had perished, took it in aversion; and to quench his thirst God created the vine, and revealed to him the means of converting its fruit into wine.[15]

Benjamin Franklin. 1779. Engraving by Louis-Jacques Cathelin after Anne-Rosalie Filleul. Reproduced by courtesy of the Franklin Collection, Yale University Library.

Noah also gave rise to the "drinking song" Benjamin Franklin penned about 1745:

> Honest old Noah first planted the Vine,
> And mended his Morals by drinking its Wine;
> And justly the drinking of water decry'd;
> For he knew that all Mankind, by drinking it dy'd. . . .
>
> From this Piece of history plainly we find
> That Water's good neither for Body nor Mind;
> That Virtue & Safety in Wine-bibbing's found
> While all that drink Water deserve to be drown'd. . . .[16]

Franklin's playful fun with scriptures often bordered on the sacrilegious. He mused that Jesus's conversion of water into wine at the marriage in Cana was intended to show us that wine is "a constant proof that God loves us, and loves to see us happy."[17] The most memorable of his theological discourses on wine was his 1779 letter to the Abbé Morellet. In a witty response to the Morellet's earlier draft of a drinking song, which suggested that the real reason for the American Revolution was Benjamin's wish to drink good French wine rather than the drab beer of the English.[18] In this letter Franklin argued that only Divine Providence could lie behind the glorious location of the elbow. He proposed that the elbow is positive proof that God desires us to drink wine. After all, had God placed the elbow either lower or higher on the arm, we would not be able to lift our wine glass directly to our mouths. His vinicultural homily summons us to acknowledge that "from the actual situation of the elbow, we are enabled to drink at our ease, the glass going directly to the mouth. Let us, then, with glass in hand, adore this benevolent wisdom;—let us adore and drink!"[19] Benjamin's grandson, William Temple Franklin, later etched a comical drawing of the calamities that humans would endure if the elbow had been placed too near the hand or too near the shoulder.

Franklin's *Autobiography* reveals much about the liberal, Enlightenment-inspired theological views that many of New England's educated men held in the Revolutionary era. Religiously educated as a Presbyterian, Franklin ultimately decided that biblically based theology was unintelligible to the rational intellect. This is not to say that he was an atheist, nor even really an agnostic. As with other "deists" of his day, he "never doubted, for instance, the existence of the Deity; that he made the world, and govern'd it by his Providence; that the most acceptable service of God was the doing of good to man; that our souls are im-

William Temple Franklin's illustrations for a letter to the Abbé Morellet. Reproduced from M. Lémontey, ed., *Mémoires de l'abbé Morellet . . .* (2 vols., Paris, 1821), I, following p. 296. Courtesy of the Franklin Collection, Yale University Library.

mortal; and that all crime will be punished, and virtues rewarded, either here or hereafter. These I esteem'd the essentials of every religion."[20] This rationally sophisticated view of religion was relatively common among "men of learning" and, therefore, among those who gathered in the upper-class men's drinking clubs to savor imported wines and to engage in lively discussion.

Thomas Jefferson is another example of the early linking of wine enthusiasm with both the "high culture" of the eastern United States and a religious outlook that ran counter to the more established theological vision of New England Puritanism. Inventor, architect, statesman, philosopher, and farmer, Thomas Jefferson was also one of the most naturally gifted wine tasters ever to have graced these shores. His palate was exceptionally discerning. For example, during his visits to vineyards in France and Germany in 1787 and 1788, he recorded in his diary that "there are four vineyards of the first quality." These four vineyards were, astonishingly enough, precisely the four later to be declared as "first growth" wines in the famous 1855 French classification. Jefferson's travel diaries abound with eloquently composed tasting notes. The framer of the Constitution and avowed religious skeptic worked diligently to stimulate American production of wines that would have the finesse and subtle qualities of distinction that characterized the great wines of Europe in his day. He tried valiantly but in vain to cultivate the many plantings of vinifera that he imported from such prestigious French wine growers as Chateau d'Yquem. Despair more than patriotism drove him to acknowledge in 1809 that Americans would be better off trying to cultivate the indigenous grape varietals rather than "losing time and effort in the search of foreign vines which it will take centuries to adapt to our soil and climate."[21]

It has been recorded that John F. Kennedy, while entertaining a group of Nobel prize winners at the White House, welcomed them as the most distinguished gathering of intellects to have dined at the Executive Mansion "with the possible exception of when Mr. Jefferson dined here alone."[22] Kennedy may or may not have been right on that account, but certainly no occupant of the White House has rivaled Jefferson for the sophistication of his wine palate. Jefferson's claim to this distinction is really unchallenged, not even by Richard Nixon, who possessed a reasonably astute wine palate.[23] Those fortunate enough to dine at the White House during the Jefferson years enjoyed bottle after bottle of the finest French wines. Further, at Monticello Jefferson in-

Thomas Jefferson, early America's most distinguished enologist. Portrait by Thomas Sully. Reprinted with permission of The American Philosophical Association.

Male drinking party in early America. Originally published in *When Will the Day Come?* (1857).

vented the dumbwaiter to bring wines from his cellar to the dining room. It is highly likely, in fact, that it was while enjoying his evening wine that Jefferson sat in front of his fireplace and used his scissors to cut apart his New Testament until it contained no more references to miracles or the supernatural. This version was, in his opinion, consequently more fit for reading by a rational person.[24]

Jefferson's rationalism in matters of religion aligned him with the most liberal religious sentiments of his day. He insisted that all theological concepts, particularly those based on an appeal to some supernatural revelation, were nothing but the "charlatanry of the mind."[25] Jefferson was, then, inclined to a "natural" rather than a revealed religious outlook. Early America's most celebrated wine enthusiast, he possessed an aesthetic sense that fostered a religious outlook that he wrote enabled him "to perceive and feel a conviction of design, consummate skill, and indefinite power in every atom [of the universe]."[26] Thus, Thomas Jefferson, the wine lover, was simultaneously one in whom intellectual complexity and a commitment to a rational explanation of the universe could coincide with an aesthetic feel for the deeper spiritual reaches of nature. Jefferson's passion for religion and for wine was thus a kind of restrained romanticism in which rational intellect and aesthetic spirituality joined together.

The examples of Franklin and Jefferson help to illustrate the fact that, beginning with our national origins, there has been a continuing tendency for wine drinking to be identified with the learned and culturally sophisticated members of American society.[27] Throughout the late eighteenth and the first half of the nineteenth centuries, wine was the beverage of choice at male dinner parties. Wine not only provided the stimulus to a felt sense of collegiality and spirited conversation, but was often itself the topic of conversation, as fellow wine enthusiasts might compare tasting notes and describe in detail their recent sensory delights.

To understand better this connection between wine consumption and highbrow American culture, we might return to studies of the social dimension of alcohol consumption. Although there is an abundance of psychological and sociological studies on motivations for drinking alcohol, two articles have emerged as classics in the field and have figured centrally in the literature produced over the last forty years. Selden Bacon's "Alcohol and Complex Society" established the thesis that alcohol's major function in modern society is to reduce tension, guilt, anxiety, and frustration.[28] Bacon also observed that alcohol consumption permits certain types of social interaction to occur that are usually barred or restricted in everyday behavior. Finally, Bacon noted that alcohol promotes a "variation in ideas." Similarly, Donald Horton's classic article, "The Function of Alcohol in Primitive Societies: A Cross-Cultural Study," also drew attention to alcohol's tendency to foster a certain spontaneity in our social and cognitive patterns.[29] Horton discovered that alcohol consumption typically meets four basic human needs: 1) hunger and thirst; 2) medicine; 3) religious ecstasy; and 4) social jollification. Horton further contended that the more complex or competitive a society is, the more important it is for there to be the kind of "social jollification" that alcohol provides so that individuals can relate to one another in noncompetitive ways.

If we are correct in our assumption that many of the American upper class were motivated to drink not to reduce their intrapsychic tensions or anxiety, but actually to increase the amount and complexity of their intrapsychic sensations, then it is reasonable to assume that wine could fulfill this need far better than distilled spirits. As fellow male wine enthusiasts joined for an evening of "jollification," they were enabled to break out of stereotypically male patterns of non-emotive, competitive interaction. Drinking wine together promoted forms of intimacy and closeness that otherwise violated social protocol for males in their various professional roles. Moreover, the aesthetic ritual of savoring wine required persons to be intellectually prepared to match sensory experience with memories of drinking similar wines in the past and with information gained through reading or conversation.[30] Wine drinking required (and still requires), among other things, an accumulated knowledge of the special characteristics of each vintage, different geographical peculiarities, and previous tastings of similar wines. As persons gathered to drink and discuss wines they gradually built upon their previous tasting experience and made new, spontaneously arrived at opinions about each wine. In all likelihood they usually found themselves engaged in political or theological discussions as well, and they argued about these matters in a manner that permitted a "variation in ideas," or spirited departures from conventional beliefs. This is, to be sure, a speculative line of interpretation. Yet, it remains a fact that wine was historically associated with the very socioeconomic classes that were also statistically more likely to subscribe to Enlightenment rationality, Unitarianism, or the more liberal wings of the Episcopal, Presbyterian, and Congregationalist denominations. Among the eastern "high culture," then, wine had a tendency to be aligned with sentiments that combated rigidity, dogmatism, and sectarian disputation. Instead, wine seems to have been a part of a distinctive cultural style that was progressive, supportive of rational self-determination, and interested in individual freedom of expression.

CHAPTER 2

Western Expansion

RELIGION AND "A HAPPY WINELAND"

American wine culture was, of course, never confined to the eastern sea-board. During the seventeenth and eighteenth centuries, however, California was under the dominion of Spain. The Spanish government was, for the most part, uninterested in the social or cultural development of the regions they called Baja (lower) and Alta (upper) California. The Spanish who ventured into this region of the New World were primarily treasure seekers, looking for gold, silver, and gems. There were, therefore, comparatively few secular pioneers interested in settling down in the region and building productive communities. As a consequence, the work of civilizing this wild new frontier fell upon the shoulders of the Roman Catholic Church. For this reason, the emerging culture—and viniculture—of California revolved around the missions established by the Jesuits and the Franciscans as they toiled to incorporate yet another pagan wilderness into the Kingdom of God on earth.[1]

The Mission Trail and California Viniculture

In 1697 Father Juan Ugarte led a small group of Jesuit priests across the Gulf into the Baja region of California. There they established a mission for the purpose of creating a center around which a Christian civilization might flourish. Ugarte immediately planted grapes so that his mission would have a reliable supply of wine for celebrating Holy Communion and a staple for the priests' otherwise frugal meals. The grape that Ugarte used for making his wines was probably the blue-black varietal of vinifera root stock that is traditionally identified as the Mission grape. Although the Mission grape makes rather flat, unspectacular wines, it is a hearty varietal and ably served the needs of the Jesuits, who needed to produce wine rapidly and dependably.

By 1708 a second mission was founded, and, within a few decades, the Jesuit order had succeeded in establishing fifteen missions in lower California. Records indicate that at least five of the fifteen were producing wine by 1760. The Society of Jesus, or Jesuits, have long been known for their zeal and military-like discipline. The difficulties of cultivating wines in this fairly barren region called forth every bit of the Jesuits' ingenuity and determination. At Mission Santa Gertrudis, for example, a mile-long irrigation tunnel had to be cut through rock to bring water to the vines from a local spring. And, too, there was a continuous shortage of suitable containers for storing wine. Earthen jugs had to be made or bartered for from trading ships. At Mission Santa Gertrudis one priest actually chopped reservoirs in rocks, filled them with wine, and then sealed them with pitch. Yet the Jesuits triumphed over the obstacles set before them and brought the active cultivation of European-style vinifera wines to the western shores of North America.

In 1769 a new surge of mission building began to the north in the Alta, or upper, California region. This second stage of mission building was led by the Franciscan order. The subsequent history of wine production and consumption in what is now the state of California was therefore shaped by the life and activity of the Franciscan friars until the middle of the nineteenth century. While the commercial sale of wine by the early Franciscans was helpful in meeting their expenses, the need for external revenues was actually a minor element in their commitment to viniculture. They were primarily interested in wine for its medicinal value in attending to the sick, for their own enjoyment at the dinner table, and for use in performing the mass. The canon law of the Catholic Church stipulates minimum standards for the quality of wine to be used at the altar.[2] In actuality, these laws merely correspond to good wine-making practices and only eliminate wines of doubtful origin or those made from careless production methods. Having a bishop's certification that one's wine was valid for celebrating the Eucharist became increasingly important as the years went on and commercial wine making began to develop in California. The Church provided a fairly sizable market and could help a winery secure a sufficient volume of sales to cover basic operating costs. This, as we shall see, has been important even into the twentieth century, as it helped keep some of California's premier wineries in operation during Prohibition.

The gradual expansion of the mission trail along the California coast throughout the 1700s and into the early 1800s was thus necessarily accompanied by the gradual dissemination of grape vines and vinicultural expertise. It was Father Junipero Serra who founded the Mission San Diego in 1769 and who is also traditionally accredited with bringing with him the Mission grape.[3] It is possible that Junipero Serra was the

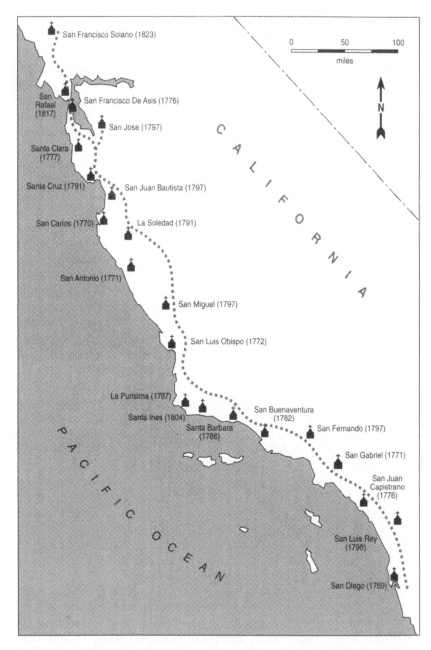

The Mission Trail and the development of major Californian viticultural regions.
Map courtesy of The University of Tennessee Cartography Lab.

most important figure in the entire history of California. No one knows for certain whether his real desire was to convert the small, scattered population to the north or whether he was at heart an adventurer seeking wild new frontiers. Whatever his motivations, Serra succeeded in opening up a splendid new territory with economic potential that far exceeded that of the mountainous deserts of what is now Mexico's Baja region. Soon after erecting the San Diego mission, Serra directed his energies northward to push the Church's influence farther up the coastline. He steadily directed the construction of a long chain of missions, each of which was soon surrounded by a thriving village.

Serra selected his sites carefully, looking for good harbors, rich valleys, beautiful vistas, and viticultural promise. San Diego, Los Angeles, Santa Barbara, Monterey, and San Francisco stand today on sites where Serra erected his missions. The twenty-first, and last, of the missions to be added to this chain was constructed at Sonoma in 1823. The road that connected these Christian outposts was known as *El Camino Real*, or King's Highway. Today that road links together California's famed wine-producing regions. Thus, the Catholic faith, by taming the California frontier in the name of religion, had quite literally sewn the seeds that would in time flower into what is perhaps the greatest wine-producing region in the world.

There is some dispute as to just when any of these missions actually succeeded in planting grapes and producing wine. Tradition has generally focused upon Gen. Mariano Vaellejo's contention that his father had reported wines being produced by Father Serra at San Diego right after its founding in 1769. Yet, as late as 1783, Father Serra's writings complained of having no wine to celebrate the mass other than unreliable shipments of wine from Mexico or Spain. The earliest documented production of wines by California missions appears to have been between 1781 and 1782 at San Juan Capistrano.[4] A few years later the mission at San Gabriel near Los Angeles emerged as the most successful producer of wines, soon producing thirty-five thousand gallons of wine per year in addition to sizable quantities of brandy. By the early 1800s it is clear that most of the missions along El Camino Real were producing sufficient quantities of wine to meet the dietary needs of the priests and to ensure the celebration of mass. Travelers in the period reported having "plenty of good wine during supper" when passing through the region, particularly from the wines of Sonoma.[5] Just how far the missions went in transforming their wine-production facilities into a commercial venture is not known, although many of the missions almost certainly sold wines to provide financial support for their religious activities. In 1833, however, the Mexican government stripped the Franciscans of their secular enterprises, and over the next two decades the commercial production of wine by the missions came to a halt. Most of the vineyards surrounding the missions fell into ruin. The demise of the missions' wine-making capabilities, however, coincided with and stimulated the growth of the secular wine-making industry in California, and thus the "Golden State" was not to be deprived of one of its most important commercial enterprises.

Some Catholic wineries, incidentally, continued to prosper into the late twentieth century. The Novitiate Winery of Los Gatos produced altar wines and some commercial wines to help support Jesuit seminary education until it finally closed operations in 1986. One of its wine makers, Father Thomas Dutton Terry, later became president of the University of Santa Clara, making him the only wine maker college president in our nation's history. A second Catholic winery, The Christian Brothers Winery, was established in 1882 and was the largest church-owned winery in the world until it sold its operations to a British corporation in 1989. Located in the southern portion of the famed Napa Valley, the Novitiate of Mont La Salle monastery trains young men to join this worldwide Catholic teaching order founded by Saint Jean Baptiste de la Salle in 1680. The Christian Brothers began making wine at their original novitiate in 1882 for their table and altar use. Soon after relocating to the Mont La Salle site in 1932, they began to expand their commercial operation. For several decades they have been the largest producers of Napa grapes and make over fifty different wines, ranging from generic table wine to premier brandies. Much of the leadership for the Christian Brothers' heritage of producing fine varietal wines came from Brother Timothy Diener, who became cellarmaster in 1936 and directed the Christian Brothers' efforts to produce some of Napa Valley's finest wines. Yet, after 107 years of financing their educational programs and other spiritual wines by producing wine, the Christian Brothers finally sold their vineyards and historic wineries to the British conglomerate, Grand Metropolitan PLC. The reasons for this sale are not wholly known. The Christian Brothers announced that they wanted to use the reported $125 million from the sale to focus on educational programs rather than on wine production. Many industry observers suspected another reason: the order's increasing moral dilemma created by widespread public concern over alcohol abuse. The neo-Prohibitionist zeal of many who have championed the anti-alcohol crusade in recent years may well have made this religious order, which for centuries had seen in wine a gracious blessing from God, uneasy about its vinicultural endeavors. Interestingly, Brother Timothy was personally troubled by those who have launched a wholesale attack on the wine industry because of alcohol

Brother Timothy Diener of Christian Brothers' Winery. Reprinted by permission of The Christian Brothers' Winery.

abuse. Quick to point out that both the grapes and the yeast that make wine are found together in the God-given order of things, Brother Timothy sought to moderate the attack on wine by those who believe wine bottles should contain printed warnings for wine's harmful effects. Widely known for his kind, loving personality, Brother Timothy spoke out sharply against those who would cast moral or spiritual aspersion upon wines and has even endorsed the distribution of T-shirts that bear his personal homily: "Christ made wine . . . miraculously from water. He attached no warning label to that wine."

When Mexico received independence from Spain, the mission properties were transferred to a Mexican government that had more important matters to attend to than the tending of either religious activities or wine production in a distant territory. The missions' vineyards predictably fell into ruin by the early 1830s. Irrigation systems fell into disrepair, vineyards were left unattended or were ripped up to make way for other crops, and winery equipment was gradually lost or thrown away. Fortunately, the demise of church-directed wine making took place at about the same time as the genesis of the region's first commercial wine making.

The commercial production of wine in California began in earnest when Jean Louis Vignes, a native of the Bordeaux region of France, brought several varietals of vinifera root stock to California and began to make and sell wines to the growing consumer market. What followed is a singularly impressive story of the role that immigrants have played in the process of "creative borrowing" whereby the United States has built upon its largely European heritage in ways that expressed its own growing cultural style. The "Who's Who" of American wine culture is almost entirely composed of first-generation immigrants.[6] It contains names such as Paul Masson, Charles Krug, the Wente brothers, Hans Kornell, George de Latour, Jacob Schramm, Mirassou, Rossi, Franzia, Concannon, Martini, and Sebastiani. It might be noted that it was the burgeoning wine industry, not gold, that built California's economy in the late 1800s. The gold rush of 1849 provided thousands of consumers for the fledgling California wine business, and the disappointed prospectors found in California wines an inexpensive pleasure in the Golden State. A good many of them were to find a steady income, if not an instant fortune, in the rapidly expanding wine industry.

The Midwestern Heritage

The combination of westward migration, religious expansion, and the profusion of viniculture also appeared in many regions between the two coasts. After all, as educated clergy moved westward into the frontier they would naturally expect the refinements of eastern society—not to mention the necessary ingredients for celebrating the Lord's Supper— to follow them. Thus, for example, in 1818 a Baptist deacon, Elijah Fay, founded the western New York wine industry by planting a vineyard, and his son, Joseph, was later to build the first winery in the area at Brocton. An Episcopalian minister, Rev. William Bostwick, is cred-

Missouri's Lutheran minister and vinicultural expert, Friedrich Muench. Reprinted by permission of the State Historical Society of Missouri, Columbia.

ited with the beginnings of the important Finger Lakes vineyards in the late 1820s. The oldest winery in Indiana, the Saint Meinrad Archabbey and Theological Seminary, to this day makes five thousand gallons of wine annually to be used at the monks' evening meals.

In Missouri, a Lutheran minister, Friedrich Muench, built a winery in 1881 and not only made acclaimed wine but also wrote a volume entitled *School for American Grape Culture* in which he tried to disseminate his vinicultural expertise. An immigrant to the New World and its midwestern frontier, Muench was convinced that "with the growth of the grape every nation elevates itself to a higher grade of civilization—brutality must vanish, and human nature progresses."[7] Muench wrote a great deal on religion and philosophy in addition to his writings on wine.[8] He was particularly drawn to Emerson's Transcendentalist beliefs, perhaps accounting for his ability to see a divine meaning and significance in such natural delights as wine. Muench foresaw great vinicultural promise in California, Ohio, Missouri, Virginia, Pennsylvania, Tennessee, and Illinois. He pointed out that increased viniculture in his own state of Missouri would add new jobs to the economy and provide previously underpaid laborers with an attractive form of labor in which they can engage "in daily intercourse with peaceful nature."[9] Also, an "obstacle to slave labor would be raised, by the extension of the new brand of freemen's industry."[10] But, above all, new settlers would find that this "luscious liquid will never be missing on festive occasions" and that they could daily enjoy this "enlivening, cheering, healthy drink."[11] Muench's continued efforts to disseminate sound grape-growing practices helped Missouri to become the second-largest wine-producing state by the latter part of the nineteenth century. The Missouri wine industry, incidentally, would have completely ended during Prohibition had it not been for two small seminaries that kept the art alive during those years.

Also influential in developing the Missouri wine industry was the religious freethinker George Husmann. Husmann's father and his elder brother were both among the original incorporators of St. Paul's Lutheran Church in Hermann, Missouri.[12] A few years after its founding the church's constitution was rewritten, with the new version declaring that the church had been called Lutheran in error. It seems that although the first members and pastor were Lutheran, the remaining members of the congregation considered themselves freethinkers, and both their religious views and their radical politics made them at odds with the organized Lutheran Church in Missouri. As Husmann grew up, he absorbed this freethinking spirit, as well as the art of wine growing practiced by a good many in this heavily German community. Although lacking much in the way of formal education, he was hired by the University of Missouri to teach horticulture. Husmann's teaching, research, and writing significantly advanced Missouri viticulture and viniculture. True to his character, Husmann's numerous publications on wine contain frequent references to his religious and philosophical views. In an address to the State Teacher's College in 1879, he stated that as a boy he had learned from his father "to look from nature up to nature's God."[13] Like most wine makers, Husmann considered wine the drink of temperance and was convinced that if Prohibition were ever to come, it would place strictures only on distilled spirits and exempt both beer and wine. Also of note is the fact that George Husmann was one of three framers of the Missouri Emancipation Ordinance in early 1865. Husmann was in this way quite typical of the many midwestern German grape growers who, although of various religious persuasions, appreciated good wines and advocated what were considered in that day quite radical political beliefs.

An important part of the settlement of the Midwest was the formation of small religious communities seeking to establish a utopian, God-centered society. And, interestingly, several of these actively embraced wine as a means of symbolizing and strengthening their communal ties. Writing in 1874, Charles Nordhoff observed that there were about five thousand people living in seventy-two communal sites across the United States.[14] Nordhoff observed that many of these groups, such as the Shakers and the Oneida community, held perfectionistic beliefs that made the consumption of alcohol a personal sin. Yet other groups, and particularly those settled by German immigrants, were actively involved with wine production. The Amana colonies in Iowa were a perfect example. The founders of the Amana colonies were German immigrants belonging to a religious sect called the Community of True Inspiration that originated as an offshoot of Lutheranism in Germany during the eighteenth century. Their identity as "inspirationalists" stemmed from their belief that the community's leaders could directly receive divine inspiration in the same manner as the biblical prophets. The claim to divine inspiration predictably led to a certain amount of ostracism and strife in Germany, prompting a modest number of them to journey to America in the mid-1800s. After their arrival in Amana ("remain true"), Iowa, in 1854, they were able to sustain a communitarian society for three generations before the Great Depression forced them to accept capitalism.[15] The seven villages that made up the original colony exist to this day as a vivid testimony to the role of faith in the settling of America's vast frontier.

The Amana colonists embraced an austere and disciplined life. These determined souls endured a great many hardships in order to separate from the secular world for the purpose of cultivating humility, faithfulness, and love of Christ. The seven villages that they erected were spaced approximately one to two miles apart. Each village had its own store, church school, bakery, dairy, livestock barns, sawmill, butcher shop, vineyard, and winery. Their German heritage was steeped in a tradition in which wine and religion were fused together in the celebration of life. A wine maker living today in Amana recounts the background that Amana's wine makers brought with them to the New World.

> Religion was a strong force behind the spread of wine-making. Monks tended vineyards and ran some of the best and certainly some of the largest wineries in Europe, where wine was part of every meal. Wine comforted the aged and the sick. It cheered and refreshed the weary. It was a gesture of friendliness and hospitality. It was a gift. It was a thank you. It sealed pledges between sweethearts and ambassadors. A cup or a glass of wine was part of the daily lives and the celebrations and festivals and feasts for the rich and the poor alike. That is how wine is still used today.[16]

The early colonists built upon and creatively transformed this heritage in their new communal setting. They found that the drinking of wine not only was perfectly consistent with but actually promoted the bonding of individuals into a community that was aimed at purifying persons so that they might serve as "instruments" or "inspired oracles" of holy spirit. In this communistic society, each family was provided with a home, food, and clothing in exchange for their work in the colony's various farming and industrial enterprises. Thus, for example, all food was prepared in large community kitchens located in each of the seven villages. The preparation of food was important to the communal life of the society. From the gathering of supplies through the cleaning up of dishes, food production was an important focal point of conversation and social interaction. Part and parcel of this sharing of bread with one another was the sharing of wine, which was dispensed from the communal kitchens at both lunch and dinner. It might be pointed out that to this day Amana wine is sold to tourists who dine in the local restaurants and to those who purchase it to bring home as a remembrance of their visit to the simple, natural ways of pious living.

Those who resided in the Amana colonies had made a conscious decision to live within a self-contained, self-sufficient, communal church society. Work hours were long and the tasks were often physically demanding. The frequent mingling of wine with these work details turned even the most menial of tasks into a celebration of one's service to God and to community. The old Amana colonies produced two kinds of wine—community wine (*geimeindschaftlicher Wein*) and family wine (*hinterlistiger Wein*).[17] The community wine was an official enterprise of the religious community. Each village had its own cellarmaster, who presided over the village's vineyards and coordinated all of the efforts at harvest time when all other work would be suspended so that men, women, and children could help bring in the new year's crop. The colonies bought the vines and wine-making equipment on the same cooperative basis as other activities in the seven villages were managed. The cellarmaster was the overseer of the wine-making activity and could count upon additional labor as the need arose. It was also the cellarmaster's duty to store properly the village's entire supply in a cellar built in the church basement and to dispense each family's wines on a periodic basis. This was no small task. Each of the seven villages produced more than six thousand gallons of community wine each year. A certain amount was given each day to the community kitchen to be served along with meals. An additional amount was allocated to each family. Each man was allotted twenty gallons of community wine each year and each woman received twelve gallons (although frequently she gave her share to her husband to drink). This was not the family's only source of wine since almost every family supplemented its thirty-two gallon allotment with its own homemade wines.

Middle Amana, Iowa, around 1900. Courtesy of Amana Heritage Society.

Wine drinking provided a sense of camaraderie and festivity to the work schedule. Each farm worker was given two wine breaks each day. Crew bosses would stop by and pick up the daily ration and be certain that every worker received no less than two ounces of wine at both their morning and afternoon breaks. (Factory workers did not have wine breaks because of the possibility of drowsiness or inattentiveness while using machinery.) Other tasks also earned extra wine rations. For example, one of the most important duties that all males had to perform on a rotating basis was that of manning the watchtower. The primary purpose of this nightly assignment was to be on the lookout for fires and intruders. The "watchtower duty" was of such vital importance to the safety of the village that the Amana colonists found innovative ways of transforming its potential drudgery or boredom into a fun-filled activity. As a rule, persons—especially teenagers—volunteered to accompany the man on duty in hope of seeing the night watch turn into a party. Others would stop by with baskets of food specially prepared by the community kitchen and including generous portions of steak and slices of pie or pieces of cake—and, of course, an extra ration of wine for all. Card playing, ordinarily frowned upon in this pious community, would often begin, and thus through each night a small group of young men would share food, wine, and one another's company all in the spirit of helping one another perform an otherwise tedious chore.

The Amana church only used wine for its annual communion service, which was called the *Liebesmahl*, or Love Feast. The Liebesmahl was the holiest of the Amana church services and was eagerly anticipated all year. The pageant-like communion was a lengthy observance and often took two Sundays to complete. In this service community members sat in small groups, and each group had one communal wine goblet. The officiating elder gave the signal for each individual to have a turn drinking from the goblet in a distinct hierarchical order determined by age, marital status, number of children, etc. The wine goblets would be continually refilled as it went from person to person since a good many were "inclined to swallow rather than taking the customary sip."[18]

In addition to the community wine, nearly every family in old Amana made its own *hinterlistiger Wein*, which roughly translates as "made on the sly." Each family made its own generous supply of wine from black currants, elderberries, wild grapes, or rhubarb. Most of the wine was made in the family cellar by men, although the few women who did become the family wine makers were reputed to be among the colony's finest. It was the family wine that was used at weddings, given as gifts, or enjoyed in the evenings or on Sundays. Sunday "wine samplings" were, in fact, rituals that went to the heart of Amana's communal fabric. Right after the Sunday worship service, the men of each Amana village would disappear from sight, reconvening at the prearranged site of the week's tasting. All dressed up in their Sunday suits and ties, the men brought some of their own homemade wine to share with others in a friendly tasting competition. Each wine was savored and critically discussed. Sunday was their one day off from the hard work of the community, and their wine samplings gave them time to engage in easy, mellow conversation to refresh themselves for the coming week.

The Amana colonies' use of wine to affirm their communal commitments and to encourage their "inspirational" form of piety almost perfectly illustrates anthropologist Mary Douglas's contention that "the meaning of a meal is found in a system of repeated analogies."[19] That is, there was a mutually reinforcing relationship between the ways in which wine was associated with religious worship, community meals, and informal social gatherings. In this way the meaning of consuming wine in any one context was embedded in a much wider system of "analogies" that accentuated its symbolic role in mediating between the individual and the community, the mundane and the extraordinary, the secular and the sacred. And, as Douglas also notes, "[E]ach meal is a structured social event which structures others in its own image."[20] The

Model of the nineteenth-century settlement in New Harmony, Indiana. Courtesy of University of Southern Indiana/Historic New Harmony.

Amana colonies, as was the case among a good many other American communal groups, utilized wine in ways that fostered pervasive patterns of social interaction that were infused by the religious emotions of love and charity.

Other nineteenth-century German religious communities also embraced wine as part of the communal heritage they sought to perpetuate in their American settlements. The Amish in the Pennsylvania Dutch region still cultivate vineyards and make wine in their homes in a tradition that goes back to their German ancestry. Mennonites share a cultural and theological heritage quite similar to that of the Amish; when the Mennonites resided in Germany, they too produced and enjoyed wine. Although some modern Mennonites do consume alcohol as a means of strictly preserving their separate religious culture, most abandoned this behavior shortly after arriving in the United States. The Aurora commune in Oregon (an offshoot of the perfectionistic Bethel community) cultivated vineyards in the Willamette Valley.

Another German communal sect that favored wine use was known as the Harmony Society. The Harmony Society was structured around the inspirational leadership of George Rapp, whose mystical spirituality and extreme pietism drew a small but committed following. Members of the Harmony Society, or Rappites, as they were frequently called, strongly anticipated the imminent return of Christ and were confident that they could establish an entire community that would live in Christian purity so that a pure remnant might be awaiting the Lord at the Second Coming. In 1804 Rapp brought about six hundred followers to Pennsylvania to set up a theocratic commune. The village they founded, Harmony, Pennsylvania, was soon bustling with several industries, including the cultivation of ten acres of vines brought with them from Germany. By 1809 the Harmonists put up a new brick building with a cellar designed for wine storage. The commune fully expected that the commercial production of wines would soon add to its thriving economy.[21] Unfortunately, the Harmonists' vines quickly died from the intemperate conditions, black rot, and probably phylloxera.

The withering of their precious vineyards prompted the Rappites to move their colony and establish New Harmony in the Wabash Valley of Indiana. There, too, they built large wine cellars and again sought to make wine production a chief industry of their communal society. Between 1815 and 1824 the colonists at New Harmony transformed central Indiana into what at the time was the nation's leading center for the commercial production of wine. Although they never succeeded in growing European varietals, travelers' reports indicate that their wines were quite drinkable. Nonetheless, by 1824 the leadership decided to abandon this site as well and return to Pennsylvania, where they built yet another town, Economy. Their Indiana village was later taken over by the followers of the utopian socialist Robert Owen, but the vineyards fell into total ruin within a year. However, the Harmony Society's new vineyards (apparently of indigenous grapes this time) thrived in the Economy settlement. Indeed, Economy continued to survive for a few decades even after Rapp's death in 1847. It should be remembered that alongside their penchant for consuming wine, the Harmonists lived a strict life devoted to making themselves morally pure in anticipation of Christ's return. A part of this perfectionist zeal was their growing tendency to denounce sexuality as pertaining only to finite existence and to make celibacy the expected norm. The amorous effects so often associated with wine consequently had little effect on the size of their community, and their membership gradually dwindled to the point of extinction.

All in all, religion aided, abetted, and in many cases took the lead in the early spread of wine culture in the United States. By the late 1860s it appeared as though wine, like religion, might become one of the truly distinctive attributes of the emerging American character. Writing in the country's heartland at Hermann, Missouri, in 1866, Prof. George Husmann wrote a book entitled *The Native Grape and the Manufacture of American Wines*. Apparently underestimating the growing militancy among those Protestants whose commitment to temperance was even then building the foundations of Prohibition, Husmann wrote that "[t]he nation is affected with grape fever. I firmly believe that this continent is destined to be the greatest wine-producing country in the world, America will be, from the Atlantic to the Pacific, one smiling and happy Wineland, where each laborer shall sit under his own vine, and none will be too poor to enjoy the purest and most wholesome of all stimulants, good, cheap, native wine."[22]

The happy Wineland Husmann prophesied would later be torn asunder by the Temperance and Prohibition movements, largely of religious parentage. Yet, even as he wrote, the "grape fever" and "wholesome stimulant" of native wine were to be found in any number of religious groups that were establishing themselves as permanent features of the American religious landscape.

CHAPTER 3

Wine and American Religious Communities

Up to this point I have focused largely on the role of religious groups in establishing and supporting American viniculture. Yet, as the experience of the Amana colonies illustrates, there are other fascinating parts to the story of religion and wine in the United States. The use—and sometimes the deliberate nonuse—of wine by various religious communities has often been a significant factor in their historical experience. All religious communities are faced with the dual need to provide members with experiences of the sacred and with experiences of communal belonging. The experience of the Amana colonies described in the previous chapter provides an almost perfect example of how the use of wine frequently becomes central to both of these elements of religious living. Wine's inherent capacity to release emotions, to induce experiences of well-being or expansiveness, and to encourage novel intellectual constructions make it a natural ally (or enemy) of religious communities. Patterns of wine use therefore typically reveal a great deal about a particular religious group's manner of appropriating ritual and theological elements of the Judeo-Christian tradition. They also tell us a great deal about how religious groups go about incorporating new members and, in turn, separating these members from "outsiders." Wine use, then, is connected with both the ritual/theological and the social/cultural dimensions of religious organizations and consequently provides an insightful perspective on the life of American religious communities.

No sphere of American cultural life has displayed more diversity, innovation, and passion than religion. There are, for example, currently over two thousand different religious groups in the United States. This historic pluralism in American religion, combined with the absence of any governmentally established religion and the relative mobility of the population, has made it possible for new and experimental forms of religion to develop and expand with astonishing rapidity. It has also created a somewhat competitive religious environment that encourages religious groups to be keenly concerned with forming and preserving distinct identities. These identities are expressed in the distinctive kinds of worship, doctrine, and moral codes with which religious groups differentiate themselves from one another. Religious groups endure over time by finding ways to define and preserve their distinctive identities; that is, they devise strategies for fostering members' sense of affiliation with the group's particular form of spirituality. Their forms of worship, theology, and moral guidelines must be sufficiently well delineated to both set them apart from competing groups and provide a specific identity around which to build group loyalty. To this extent religious groups in the United States are continually engaged in what social scientists call the "boundary-setting" behaviors through which members of any group foster internal cohesiveness and learn to distinguish between in-group and out-group membership.[1]

From a sociological perspective, most religious groups in the United States have historically gravitated toward a fairly common or "mainstream" identity. Others, however, offer interpretations of religious faith that, although essentially rooted in the culture's dominant belief system, nonetheless vary in some unique and identifiable ways. Still other groups make radical breaks with conventional concepts concerning worship, belief, or lifestyles and consequently form an identity that exists—at least in their formative period—at the margins of mainstream culture. Scholars in the field of religious studies have struggled to develop terminology to describe or classify religious groups that will convey some sense of a group's social and historical proximity to the "center" of American culture. The terms denomination, sect, and cult are used to provide beginning reference points concerning a religious group's general location within the larger culture. None of the terms has a precise or consistent meaning. The purpose of these terms is not evaluative; it is simply to provide a shorthand way of locating a group in the larger religious landscape and thereby to help draw attention to the kinds of social and theological factors influencing a group's historical experience. Regardless of the definitions assigned to designations such as denomination, sect, and cult, any given religious group will have characteristics that will cut across two or more of these categories. Yet, even though these terms are inherently limited in applicability, they nonetheless help alert us to the social dynamics underlying the formation of religious groups.

Wine and Denominational Identities

We generally refer to a religious group as a denomination when its members adhere to a style of religiosity that conforms to our country's dominant social and cultural patterns. The social and cultural life of the United States has, of course, been historically linked with the Judeo-Christian heritage. More specifically, it has been a distinct core of Protestant Christian groups (e.g., Congregationalists, Presbyterians, Baptists, Methodists, Episcopalians, Disciples of Christ, and Lutherans) that have shaped the basic patterns of religion in America. It also makes sense to consider Roman Catholicism and each of the three major branches of Judaism (Orthodox, Conservative, and Reform) as denominations, since they have for many decades existed as established and viable competitors in the American religious marketplace.[2] From a sociological perspective, these latter religious groups have all established themselves within American culture and, with the possible exception of certain branches of Orthodox Judaism, have adopted patterns of religious life that allow their members to participate fully and freely in American culture. Not only are these groups "mainstream" in the sense that their members are at home in the wider American culture, they also exist more or less peacefully alongside one another. Put differently, their distinctive patterns of worship and community formation produce minimal boundary conflict. Yet each surely competes for members in the religious marketplace. And each is continually faced with the problem of socializing a new generation into its distinctive approach to the Judeo-Christian tradition. The very term *denomination* indicates that each of these groups has over time become identified with (or named for) a distinctive understanding of worship, doctrine, and everyday lifestyle by which it differentiates itself from competing forms of the Judeo-Christian tradition. These groups owe their historical success to the fact that their members feel meaningfully connected to their particular religious identity. The use of wine, as we shall see, has factored significantly into the ritual, doctrinal, and sociocultural identities of America's most historically dominant denominations.

It is important to note that the ritual use of wine has been central to the formation of a worshipping community since early biblical times. The holy scriptures of ancient Judaism make clear that wine is a sign of God's blessing and that we are to enjoy the "gladdening of the heart" that it makes possible. Wine was used by ancient Israelite priests to consecrate the altar when making sacrifices to God. And, as we shall see, wine remains an essential element of such sacred activities as the Sabbath dinner ceremony and the Seder meal at Passover.

When the first Jewish converts to the new religion of Christianity began to hold separate services, they included a sacramental meal of bread and wine, the Eucharist (the Greek word for "thanksgiving"). This service, which was chiefly celebrated on Sunday mornings, was a

Catholic priest offering mass.
Photo by Duane Zehr.

memorial of the death and resurrection of Jesus and an anticipation of
the arrival of a new Messianic Age. Christians believe that Jesus ate a
last supper with his closest disciples on the night before he died. Paul
explains in 1 Corinthians that during that meal Jesus took bread, blessed
and broke it, and gave it to his disciples, saying, "This is my body which
is for you." Jesus is said to then have taken a cup of wine, blessed it, and
pronounced that "[t]his cup is the new covenant in my blood." He then
commanded his followers to "do this in remembrance of me," and to
this day Christians continue to break bread and drink wine in the ceremony variously referred to as the Eucharist or the Lord's Supper.

Throughout history Christians have arrived at quite different interpretations of this religious ceremony. Some have viewed the equation
of bread and wine to Jesus's body and blood more literally or realisti-
cally, while others have interpreted this more symbolically. In the West,
the realistic interpretation has been the more normative, or official, interpretation as it has been articulated by Roman Catholic theologians.
Medieval theologians, for example, explained the Eucharist as the re-
enactment of the sacrifice of the Cross. They demonstrated how every

gesture in this ceremony had a direct relationship to the drama of Jesus's death and resurrection, and they further sought to explain precisely how the bread and wine were transformed into the very body and blood of Christ. The Roman Catholic theory as to how this transformation occurs is known as the doctrine of transubstantiation (from a Latin term for "change in substance"). The doctrine of transubstantiation makes use of the distinction that Aristotle made between the substance of a thing (its essence) and its accidents (its appearance, taste, etc.). Medieval theologians used this logical distinction to argue that the accidents of the wine (i.e., its sight, taste, aroma, etc.) remain the same, but its substance changes into the actual blood of Christ. The important point here is that in the Western world, religion viewed wine as fraught with mystery and magic. In some mysterious way wine possesses an essence that can be sacramentally linked with the redemptive spirit of Christ.

Many of the leaders of the Protestant Reformation modified the traditional Catholic view of transubstantiation. The reasons for this are complex. Some reasons were theological and others political; all, however, were connected with Protestantism's early efforts at creating and maintaining a distinctive religious identity. Although Reformation leaders such as Luther, Zwingli, Calvin, Brucer, and Cranmer differed on many points, their new conception of faith led them to agree on radically severing the relationship of the Eucharist to the Roman Catholic penitential system. The practical implication of their new theological views was to undercut the Catholic Church's position that its ordained priests—and only its ordained priests—are empowered to perform the actions needed to make Christ's forgiving presence available to individual human beings. Other factors that led to Protestantism's break with the "transubstantiation" view pertained to changing views of the individual's relationship to God, renewed efforts to return Christian practice to the letter of scripture, and increasing intellectual pressures to accommodate Christianity to the rising spirit of secularism (and its tendency to renounce supernaturalistic modes of thinking) spawned by Renaissance humanism. The Swiss reformer Huldreich Zwingli maintained that the bread and wine signify the body and blood, but that they do not literally possess Christ's humanity, because he had already ascended to be seated at the right hand of the Father and could thus not be physically present in these worldly objects. For Zwingli, wine is a reminder that makes Christ "present to the contemplation of faith," but it does not become transformed into the blood of Christ in any literal sense. Luther differed from Zwingli and insisted that bread and wine are in fact the vehicle, or medium, through which Christ is present to the believer. Although denying the concept of the full transubstantiation of bread and wine, Luther still insisted that these substances are the means through which Christ fulfills his promise to be truly present to the faithful. In Luther's view, the substance of Christ is present "in, with, and under" the consecrated bread and wine. On this matter John Calvin took a position that did not coincide precisely with either Zwingli or Luther. For Calvin, Christ is not actually present in or under the bread and wine used in the Eucharist. Instead, this service is said to mystically elevate the congregation into participation in the heavenly reality of Christ, who is understood to be "with" the bread and wine. Thus, although the Protestant heritage that has dominated so much of American cultural history did pull back from the Catholic view of transubstantiation, it continued to view wine as a vehicle to open up the believer's contemplation of faith and elevate the believer to a vivid sense of Christ's redemptive spirit. Wine continued to define Protestant groups as worshipping Christian communities and partaking of wine continued to signify an individual's incorporation into a distinct community of believers.

The range of Jewish and Christian groups that were to form the "religious center" of American culture, then, were heirs to a long heritage that acknowledges wine to have a unique association with the gracious spirit of God. Of historical importance is the fact that the two most dominant denominations in colonial New England were the Presbyterians and Congregationalists, each of which developed out of the Puritan wing of European Protestantism. The Puritans were those Protestants who were literally trying to "purify" the Church of England and insisted that, in England, the Protestant Reformation had not gone far enough. The Puritans maintained that the Church of England (and its American branch, the Episcopal Church) had not sufficiently rid itself of the "outer trappings" associated with Roman Catholicism. They believed that there was still too much emphasis placed upon rituals and ornate ceremonies. Too little emphasis was being given to plain Bible reading and Bible preaching. Religious life in the United States was thus originally dominated by a relatively nonliturgical tradition in which scriptural reading and Bible-based sermons took the place of sacraments and ritual as the focus of Christian worship.

Part and parcel of the liturgical and theological "boundary setting" by which these denominations differentiated themselves from Catholicism and the Church of England was a slightly revised attitude toward the meaning and significance of wine. The long-term cultural consequences would prove significant. On the one hand, even given their Puritan leanings, the most culturally dominant Protestant denominations (Congregationalists, Presbyterians, Baptists, Methodists, etc.) used wine in conducting the Lord's Supper. The theories of Luther, Calvin, and particularly Zwingli shaped Americans' views concerning Christ's presence "with" the bread and wine used in Christian worship. Simultaneously, however, the antiritual leanings of American Protestantism implicitly favored what might be called an ascetic (i.e., emphasizing self-discipline and following moral laws even at the sacrifice of personal pleasure) as opposed to aesthetic (i.e., emphasizing experiences that open the self to "higher" or nonmaterialistic influences) understanding of religion. Throughout the nineteenth century the nonliturgical and evangelical wing of Protestant thought continued to grow and eventually prompted a sizable number of Americans to make a commitment to moral perfection that required them to eliminate wine from their worship services and to denounce those who continued to use wine whether for personal delight or for the worship of God. We will return to this "countervailing" tendency among some conservative Protestant groups to define themselves through their deliberate nonuse of wine later both later in this chapter and again in chapter 4.

It is interesting to note that as the years passed, members of the Congregational, Presbyterian, and Episcopal Churches were all more likely to have access to formal education and to occupy the most influential social and economic positions in American culture. This would mean that they (along with members of Reform Judaism by the middle of the twentieth century) were statistically much more likely than their ascetic/evangelical counterparts to become exposed to the intellectual influences and modern lifestyles that promoted secular or unsupernatural ways of thinking. It would be among individuals from these historically predominant denominations that would be most likely to participate in the "wine revolution" and the form of "popular religion" such as we will examine in the last chapter.

Episcopalianism, Lutheranism, and Roman Catholicism are also to be included in the cultural mainstream of American religious history, although Lutheranism and especially Catholicism had to overcome their status as immigrant faiths before finally enjoying significant numerical and social influence. All three of these denominations are more liturgical and ritualistic than the Puritan-leaning Protestant groups that preceded them in becoming members of what might be called the "religious establishment" in the United States. It is, in fact, interesting to speculate concerning the extent to which these groups' ritualistic style of worship (and more overt identification of wine with the presence of Christ) has symbolized their slight distance from the historical "core" of American religious life, which has, at least until recently, been dominated by the nonliturgical Protestant groups. The point here is that a religious group's distance from the theological and sociological mainstream is reflected in the emphasis it puts upon the use (or nonuse) of wine. The Episcopal Church, the American branch of the Anglican Communion of Churches, has preserved the ritualistic heritage that the Anglican Church retained after separating from the Roman Catholic Church. During colonial times, Episcopalians tended to be members of America's upper class and were frequently associated with Tory politics. The denomination's historic connection with above average levels of education and income cast an aura of nonegalitarianism around it until well into the twentieth century. Not surprisingly, in the early stages of the Prohibition movement many Episcopalians found themselves in open conflict with the growing number of other Protestants who insisted that wine be removed from Christian worship. In short, the slightly greater emphasis that Episcopalians place upon ritual simultaneously reflects the slight degree to which they have historically stood apart from the Protestant "core."

Lutherans brought their liturgical tradition with them from Germany and Sweden during large waves of immigration. Arriving as non-English-speaking immigrants, Lutherans were socially "set apart," even though their theological heritage was by definition at the heart of Protestantism. Their continued use of wine both for religious worship and occasional refreshment, even during the height of Prohibition, reveals their sociological distance from the Anglo-Saxon Protestant groups, who resented the degrading presence of intemperance among so many of the immigrants to their land. Finally, Roman Catholicism has only in recent years emerged from its earlier status as the faith of an immigrant people to become the single largest religious group in the United States. The continuing immigration of Irish, Polish, German, and Italian Catholics throughout the nineteenth and early twentieth centuries greatly transformed the American religious and cultural scene. The highly ritualized Mass has, of course, been the key focus of Roman Catholic worship for centuries and clearly differentiated Catholicism from the many American Protestant groups. As the next chapter makes clear, the resentment against wine was in many respects a resentment against the presence of these foreign peoples and their foreign style of Christian worship. Yet, importantly, the liturgical traditions of Episcopalianism, Lutheranism, and Roman Catholicism kept the association of wine and spirituality present in what might be called America's "symbolic universe." These groups had enough influence upon American cultural values that in 1920 Congress amended Prohibition legislation to permit religious organizations to continue to use wine for sacramental purposes.

Wine in the Life of a Religious Community:
The Example of American Judaism

Every religious community, as has been noted, has the dual task of providing its members with a felt sense of the sacred and a felt sense of
communal belonging. From the earliest of biblical times, wine has been
the beverage most intimately associated with the rituals whereby Western religious groups have engaged in the worship of God and have celebrated their communal heritage. Wine has also brought a certain sacred quality to bear upon the significant rites of passage that individuals
face in their journey through life. The presence of wine at baptisms,
confirmations, marriages, and funeral services signifies the important
sense in which each stage of a person's life takes place in and through
membership in a worshipping community.

American Judaism provides an instructive example of the ways in
which wine drinking sustains a religious group's heritage and incorpo-
rates each new generation into a distinct denominational identity. Judaism was a relatively late arrival on American shores. Even by 1825
there were only a half-dozen active congregations in the United States;
by the Civil War there were still perhaps only fifty. By the middle and
late nineteenth century the American Jewish population steadily grew
to approximately 250,000. Under the leadership of Isaac Mayer Wise,
the liberal, or Reform, branch of Judaism emerged as the most dominant Jewish denomination. Reform Judaism, as is the case with liberal
religions generally, seeks to accommodate biblical faith to the modern
era. One important example of this effort to accommodate Jewish faith
to the modern world is that Reform Judaism looks at much of Jewish
dietary law as irrelevant to modern faith. That is, the kosher dietary
laws described in the Talmud are considered to be the product of rabbinical reasoning in a bygone era and to have no real importance in our
own time. As a consequence, the first branch of Judaism to establish
itself in America gave little thought to whether their foods were purchased or prepared in ways that adhered to traditional conceptions of
moral and religious purity. Thus, the need for distinct "kosher" wines
to be used in Jewish religious observances is not as historically critical
to America's Reform tradition as it has been in the Conservative or Orthodox traditions. To be sure, however, wine is nonetheless important
to Jewish culture and its perpetuation through ritual activities preserved
within the home and in formal services performed in the temple. And,
too, many Reform and religiously liberal Jews have participated in the
growth of interest in wine during the 1970s, 1980s, and 1990s.

Between 1880 and 1930 perhaps as many as 2.5 million Jews immigrated to America. The complexion of American Judaism altered drastically in these years since the new wave of immigrants was far more likely to affiliate with Conservative or Orthodox synagogues. Orthodox Judaism and, to a lesser extent, Conservative Judaism are very concerned that the foods they eat meet the strict requirements of kosher dietary laws. Moreover, these first-generation immigrants were understandably concerned about preserving their heritage amidst the American melting pot by continuing their distinctive cultural and religious customs. These groups have thus been more instrumental than Reform Judaism in creating a market for "kosher" wines, a subject we will return to shortly.

All three denominations of American Judaism place great importance upon the hallowing of life through religious observances both in the home and in the synagogue or temple. And central to this heritage of celebration and worship is the drinking of wine. Unlike many temperance-minded Protestant Bible scholars, Jewish scholars would never think of insisting that scripture must really be referring to unfermented grape juice, not wine. Jewish scripture is replete with passages extolling wine's virtues as a blessing from God that makes glad the hearts of men and women. In ancient times wine was used as a libation that was spread out upon the altar as an act of consecration and sanctification to prepare for worship of God. This "hallowing" function of wine continues in a symbolic way down to today. Wine is considered a symbol of joy in Jewish culture and is almost always present when something in life is to be celebrated or a memory is to be cherished. The classical Jewish toast before drinking wine is the simple phrase "To Life!"[3] This short prayer or hope expresses the Jewish reverence for the sanctity of human life and reveals why wine is present as a major symbol of sanctification in the family's Sabbath meal, at the Seder meal during Passover, at a bris—or circumcision ceremony—and at weddings.[4]

Beginning at sundown on Friday evening, the Sabbath symbolizes Jewish belief in the divine origin of all of life's blessings. The Sabbath observance traditionally begins in the home with a meal at which the entire family is gathered to give thanksgiving and to draw attention to the presence of the holy in their lives. The male head of the household then holds a cup full of wine in his hands and offers the *kiddush,* or Sabbath prayer of sanctification. The kiddush is intended to make the occasion a festive one. After reciting the prayer, wine is then shared and consumed by everyone in attendance, including children. In addition to the kiddush's role in fulfilling the biblical commandment to remember the Sabbath and to sanctify it, it is also a ceremony that symbolizes the role of the father as a spiritual guide to his children. The festivity of the weekly event helps bring a ritual structure to the fabric

Friday evening sabbath meal. Photo by Duane Zehr.

of family life and to kindle family cohesion amidst a world in which Jews are a religious minority.

The Seder meal during Passover is perhaps Judaism's most important ritual for preserving its distinct cultural history. The meal, served on the first night of Passover, is always a festive one in which family and friends gather for a rich retelling of Judaism's sacred memories. A strict requirement of the meal is that there be enough wine to fill each person's cup four times (with the cup containing at least 3.3 ounces). Also, a separate cup is set out for Elijah, symbolizing hope for the Messianic Age.

The circumcision ceremony, or bris, is likewise a hallowed occasion. The traditional blessing over the wine is said when the eight-day-old baby's name is announced. A piece of cotton is then dipped into the wine and put between the infant boy's lips so that he will relax and have the benefit of this natural anesthetic. When the circumcision is completed, the wine is also brought to the mother so that she may drink from it and recite the blessings herself. The presence and centrality of wine symbolizes the celebration of the ceremony. Innumerable toasts, along the lines of "may you have pleasure in your children and your children's children, and in their children," are offered. The event signifies the important fact that God is increasing the number of his chosen. The bris is an outward testimony that God's people are fulfilling their part of the covenant with God and that joy and honor are to be theirs as they move yet one step nearer to the fulfillment of God's promise of the restoration of a true Kingdom of God on earth. Robert Bales's study of the significance of wine in Jewish rituals notes that during a bris, "the cup of wine may be considered a visible symbol and seal of the completed act of union, and in its significance as 'The word of God,' 'the commandment of the Lord,' may be conceived as representing His part in the covenant. On this symbolic level there appears to be at least a partial identification of the moral community and its norms with Jehovah and His Commandments, with the wine serving as the concrete symbol of both. . . ."[5]

Weddings also commemorate the ongoing prosperity and harmony of the Jewish faith. The blessing and drinking of wine throughout the service sanctify the ceremony whereby the bride and groom enter into a new stage in their covenant with God and with their religious community. During the ceremony the rabbi blesses a cup of wine and hands it to the bride and groom, who each take a sip before passing it on to the closest relatives. It is also customary for the groom to break a wine glass by crushing it on the floor with his feet. Although any number of explanations of the significance of this act have been proposed, its origins and initial meaning have become obscure.

The essential uses of wine to commemorate these rites of passage and religious observances have been fairly uniform over the centuries. The cumulative effect of this ritualization of wine drinking has, as Robert Bales observes, rendered wine

> symbolic of the *sacred source of moral authority*, God and the commandments of God, the law, the moral community and those who stand for it, such as the father; the act of drinking has the ritual significance of *creating, manifesting, or renewing a union* between the individual and the source of moral authority; . . . [every pious Jew] associates the act of drinking (consciously or not) with these profoundly moving ideas and sentiments regarding the sacred and his relationship to it, because of the intimate integration of the meaningful act with the earliest processes of socialization, the rites de passage, the weekly and yearly cycle of religious events, and the relationships of individuals within the family.[6]

The concern that the wines used for these ceremonies be "kosher" reveals Judaism's ongoing effort to maintain moral and religious purity. Jewish dietary laws, called *kashruth*, originated at least in part as a cultural minority's means of maintaining an identity as a "separate" culture even while existing in predominantly non-Jewish societies. As the cultural anthropologist Mary Douglas has pointed out, a religious group's beliefs about purity and impurity invariably represent an extreme concern with protecting the social boundaries that separate its members from straying into the outside world.[7] This would seem to be true in connection with American Judaism's attitudes toward wine. As suggested above, Reform Judaism considers all wine that meets governmental health regulations to be acceptable for religious observance and, of course, is quite self-conscious about interpreting Judaism in ways that enable its members to participate fully in the broader scope of American life. Many Conservative (or Traditionalist) Jews also consider all wine to be kosher and do not believe that any rabbinical certification is necessary to consider a wine pure for everyday or Sabbath consumption.[8] Yet, for Passover most Conservative Jews use only certified kosher wines. In this sense Conservative Judaism's attitudes toward wine mirror its sense of balancing accommodation to the full scope of American culture with an active effort to preserve some sense of separate social and religious identity. Orthodox Judaism insists that wines be certified as kosher, and it is also the branch of Judaism that most clearly seeks to preserve its separate heritage over and against the larger cultural environment.

For a wine to be considered kosher in a stricter sense, it must be made under the strict supervision of a rabbi, and a Sabbath-observant Jew must take responsibility for handling the wine at each stage of its production. Wines intended for Passover must be certified to be free of any grain products and are typically marked with a "P." A winery operating according to kosher requirements must use separate crushers, tanks, and bottling machinery to insure that the wines be hygienic and pure, from the picking of the grapes to the final bottling. Wines that have been properly supervised may put the rabbi's *hechsher* seal on the label. The major principle entailed in the rabbinical supervision is that it is traditionally considered forbidden for a Jew to drink wine made or handled by a non-Jew. In ancient times this proscription safeguarded Jews from using wine made by heathens. Since it was believed that heathens made wine for the purpose of offering libations to their idols, the leaders of the ancient Jewish community prohibited any use of heathens' wine or even any Jewish-produced wine that heathens had handled. Of course, in contemporary America the concern with avoiding wine meant for idol worship is no longer relevant. The prohibition is still maintained among Orthodox and some Conservative Jews, however, "in order to prevent the kind of social conviviality, usually associated with the drinking of wine, which might lead to intermarriage of a Jew with a non-Jew."[9] It might be noted that there is also one kind of kosher wine, called Mevushal wine, that may be served by an individual (such as a waiter at a restaurant) who is not strictly kosher. Mevushal wines must, however, undergo a pasteurization process that potentially destroys many of the wine's flavors and subtle qualities.

Kosher wines are produced in Israel and at several wineries in the United States.[10] A Napa Valley winery run by a group of graduates from the University of California at Davis's renowned wine-making program produces vintage-dated kosher varietals under the label of *Hagafen* (Hebrew for "the vine"). There are several kosher wineries in the state of New York, notably Monarch in Brooklyn, Schapiro's in New York City, and Royal (*Kedem*) in Milton. Most Americans have no real idea what the word kosher means. Wine historian Leon Adams speculates that the term "kosher wine" is generally misinterpreted to mean the distinct flavor found in the two leading commercial brands—Manischewitz and Mogen David. Each of these wines is made from the sweet red Concord grape and consequently has a taste that appeals to any number of non-Jewish Americans who have grown up accustomed to sweet grape juices and soda pop. Interestingly, both of these well-known brands of kosher wine originated more or less by accident.[11] Leo Star, the son of a Polish cantor, joined a Jewish congregation during Prohibition in order to be certified to bottle kosher port and sherry. After repeal of the Eighteenth Amendment, his market shrank considerably, leaving him with little more than a small Passover trade, for which he bottled a very sweet Concord wine called Mount Zebo. In 1934 sales were so low that he was forced to accept returns from retailers. Yet, the next year he found himself swamped with reorders. Star did not realize that most of the new demand was from non-Jewish customers and erroneously concluded that his wines were selling because they met Jewish kosher dietary restrictions. Eager to maintain this image, Star entered into an agreement with the well-known Manischewitz firm to bottle his wines under its name. By the 1960s, sales of red kosher Concord wine grew to about ten million gallons per year. Manischewitz retained about a third of this market, competing principally with Mogen David (advertised as "the wine like Grandma used to make"), which itself emerged by accident when the Chicago Wine Corporation once found itself with no salable inventory except a batch of sweet red Concord wine left over from the previous Passover.

Judaism's historic ritualization of wine drinking is thus deeply rooted in its efforts to define the theological and social boundaries of group

Examples of contemporary kosher wines. Photo by Duane Zehr.

membership. It is even possible, for example, that the gradual incorporation of moderate wine drinking during religious ceremonies during
the biblical era was instrumental in displacing the pagan gods who were
frequently worshipped in orgiastic drinking ceremonies.[12] Robert Bales
has argued quite persuasively that the ritualization of drinking in Jewish religious ceremonies creates powerful sentiments and symbols of social control that account for the statistically insignificant degree of alcoholism and hedonistic drinking among contemporary Jews.[13] According to
Bales, the extensive ritualization of drinking in Jewish religious ceremonies instills a "generalized ritual attitude" in Jews' attitudes toward drinking alcohol. The ritualization of drinking thereby brings attitudes toward
alcohol within the sphere of powerful social controls and moral sentiments, thereby minimizing the danger of problem drinking. Charles
Snyder, however, goes further than Bales and suggests that there are
other sociological factors that militate against intemperance among
Jews.[14] In particular, Snyder contends that Judaism's ceremonial uses of
alcohol are connected with the group's continuing experience as a religious and ethnic minority that possesses strong socializing mechanisms.
Religious and moral prohibitions against drunkenness are, in effect,
"boundary-setting" behaviors that are needed to minimize censure from
powerful majorities and to preserve social and moral "distance" from
Gentile society.

From Use to Nonuse:
Countervailing Protestant Identities

The examples of Judaism, Roman Catholicism, Lutheranism, and Episcopalianism all dramatize how fully wine is associated with American "denominational" religious life. Further, while each of these groups has steadily warned against the dangers of alcohol abuse, each has nonetheless helped foster attitudes toward personal conduct and healthy living that include the possibility of enjoying wine's "gladdening of the heart." Other mainstream American denominations, however, have had a historic wariness about the consumption of alcohol that extends to the drinking of wine. Baptist, Methodist, and most Disciples of Christ Churches are heirs to what might be called the "ascetic" strand of Protestant Christianity. From the outset many Protestants of the ascetic strand believed that self-discipline, including self-denial, was critical to religious piety. The founder of Methodism, John Wesley, connected the pursuit of spiritual holiness with strict adherence to regimens designed to promote physical and mental health. Thus, in the very middle of his treatise on Christian perfection that appeared in *General Rules of the United Societies,* Wesley included long discussions of food, drink, exercise, and sharply phrased strictures against self-indulgence and the drinking of distilled spirits.[15] During the eighteenth and nineteenth centuries, many Methodists condoned "moderate drinking," particularly of beer and wine. But as the temperance movement gained momentum in the late 1800s, Methodists were among the vanguard of those calling for total abstinence. Ardent prohibitionists, Methodists worked diligently to secure the passage of constitutional amendments at both the state and national levels to prohibit the sale or transportation of alcoholic beverages.[16] It was thus no coincidence that, as the next chapter will show, it was a Methodist by the name of Dr. Thomas Welch who saw it as his sacred vocation to manufacture unfermented grape juice for the purpose of conducting the Lord's Supper without the taint of moral evil.

Baptists, too, have historically opposed the consumption of alcohol in any form. Because Baptists witnessed their greatest growth on the ever-expanding American frontier, many of their members had little choice but to consider alcohol a necessary part of their diet and an important part of medical treatment. Yet, throughout the nineteenth century, temperance became increasingly associated with Baptists' moral outlook. Various Baptist groups were among the very first to endorse temperance organizations, such as the Anti-Saloon League, and early prohibition legislation. Like the Methodists and Disciples of Christ,

Baptists have tended to supplement their moral and religious objections to alcohol consumption (including wine drinking) with both medical and social arguments. Believing that alcohol is bad for health and disastrous to family life, Baptists have steadfastly preached against the use of alcohol in all of its forms.[17] It should be noted, however, that Baptists have a democratic and decentralized polity, and thus each believer has the right to come to his or her own opinion on such matters. One recent study showed that 48 percent of Southern Baptists drink alcoholic beverages despite strong pressure from the pulpit and denominational authorities.[18]

A very similar pattern can be found in the history and present experience of the Disciples of Christ.[19] Early Disciples commonly spoke against the use of alcohol, but by the late 1800s the cause of temperance became a near obsession. As one Disciple leader put it, even "the question of slavery was never anything but a baby by the side" of the prohibition of alcohol.[20] The Disciples of Christ, like the Baptists and Methodists, have historically promulgated theories of health and well-being that warn against using alcohol because it led to moral, physical, and social infirmity. Yet, like the Baptists and Methodists, many of the denomination's members have, over the years, opted for personal habits at variance with its official teachings.

Baptists, Methodists, and Disciples of Christ—much like the various holiness and Pentecostal denominations, such as the Assemblies of God or Church of the Nazarene, that have displayed great vitality in the late twentieth century—are rooted in the evangelical wing of American Protestantism. Evangelicalism emphasizes the importance of faith (i.e., correct belief) over religious or moral works in securing salvation. American evangelical groups typically see salvation as dependent upon an individual's conscious, willed decision to accept Jesus as one's personal Savior. Emotionalism is a strong element in evangelical religion, but mainly as a factor intended to culminate in a distinct conversion experience. These faiths have, in fact, spread throughout the American population principally by using revivalistic methods to elicit powerful human emotions and simultaneously directing those emotions toward structured religious conversions. Yet, from a theological point of view, these evangelical denominations affirm that emotions themselves cannot bring one to salvation any more than moral or religious works. It is only the grace of Christ received through faith that brings salvation. Evangelical faiths are consequently wary of alcohol because of its ability to release the wrong emotions or prevent the emotions from being properly centered on what ought to be their true object. It is also important to note that American evangelical faiths, while emphasizing that works are not the *means* of salvation, nonetheless proclaim that a disciplined obedience to the moral law must necessarily *follow upon,* or *result from,* salvation. A good many conservative Protestant denominations are therefore typically aligned with moral asceticism and thus encourage the subordination of most emotions (particularly those associated with worldly pleasures) to the moral will. Because alcohol releases emotions potentially at variance with a completely self-disciplined body and character, it is to be avoided as inconsistent with the actions of a person who has been regenerated by the saving grace of Christ.

Wine, then, has been a significant factor in American denominations' religious identities. It is central to the family and congregational rituals that perpetuate Jewish identity, particularly for those who seek out kosher wines in order to ensure a tradition of separation and holiness. Wine is also at the central core of the theological and liturgical changes through which Protestantism historically separated itself from Catholicism and, in turn, through which different Protestant denominations separated themselves from one another. From a theological and ritual perspective, mainstream Protestant denominations in the United States can be classified according to whether they tend to embrace a predominantly ascetic approach to religion or a primarily aesthetic approach. Because the ascetic style emphasizes self-denial and disciplining the will, this approach to religion has typically advocated complete abstinence from alcohol. On the other hand, the aesthetic style of spirituality emphasizes the role of sacraments in mediating spiritual influences and, as a consequence, has a greater appreciation for cultivating an inner receptivity to subtle, spiritual sensations. It has therefore been among those individuals and denominations drawn to the more aesthetic approach to religion that the religious and personal use of wine has tended to flourish.

There are also important sociological differences between Christian denominations that help account for their differing uses of wine. Particularly in the twentieth century, Catholicism and most mainstream Protestant denominations (e.g., Presbyterians, Congregationalists, Episcopalians, Lutherans, and members of more affluent Methodist churches) have tended to be at home in American society. These groups are considered mainstream at least partially for the reason that their members have generally accommodated themselves to the larger intellectual and social patterns of American culture. These groups are, therefore, relatively unsuspicious about the kinds of emotions or intellectual tendencies released by the mild consumption of alcohol. They have little concern about any kind of "emotional expansiveness" that might result from activities such as moderate drinking. The more ascetic groups (e.g.,

Southern Baptists, Assemblies of God, Seventh-Day Adventists, members of less affluent Methodist or Disciples of Christ churches), however, have historically espoused a more separatist stance toward American culture. The most theologically conservative and morally ascetic religious groups have consciously embraced a certain "over and againstness" in relation to the main currents of modern intellectual and social life. For this reason they are also likely to be wary of activities that might strengthen emotions or tendencies to affiliate with corrupting influences in modern society. Even the moderate consumption of alcohol, then, potentially erodes the separatist sociological commitment that is often central to membership in the more ascetic Protestant religious faiths.

Wine and Sectarianism

The American religious experience has given rise to any number of variant faiths that, while rooted in the "Protestant-Catholic-Jew" tradition, have nonetheless developed in quite original ways. The term sect, in contrast to the term denomination, is intended to draw attention to the important ways in which some religious groups self-consciously differentiate themselves from the more socially dominant forms of the tradition to which they belong. The term sect was developed by Ernst Troeltsch in his study of European religious groups that were separated from the state church. Because the United States, with the exception of certain states in the early history of the nation, has never had an established church, this term is not wholly applicable to American religious history. Nonetheless, many historians of American religion have found the term useful to describe the different historical experience of those groups whose beliefs and practices do not clearly parallel the religious and cultural mainstream. Sydney Ahlstrom, for example, uses the term in his highly regarded *A Religious History of the American People* as a conceptual device for accentuating common characteristics of religious innovation in American history.[21] Ahlstrom suggests that variant faiths are typically founded by an individual who possesses an extraordinarily influential personality. This leader instills a certain enthusiasm or style into the group that becomes embodied in the emerging tradition. Also, whereas a denominational affiliation is often inherited at birth from one's parents' religious heritage, sectarian membership is more likely to be the product of a conscious decision by an adult. New members have typically gone through some experience that inducts them into the group's distinctive ethos and imparts to them a conviction of having acquired a new identity. Other features that have tended to be associated with sectarian commitment in American religious history are communal living, a hunger for intense personal religious experience, a strong concern with ongoing moral perfection, and an enthusiastic expectation of the imminent return of Christ and the end of the world as we know it. Of course, not all of these defining characteristics of sectarian piety would be present in any one group. But together they help to identify those styles of religiosity that set certain religious groups apart from more conventional religious affiliations.

Both the use and the prohibition of wine among American religious sects shed additional light on the dynamics of religious innovation. For example, the use of wine draws our attention to the role of altered states of consciousness in facilitating prototypically religious feelings such as awe, surrender, or ecstasy. Wine's tendency to promote "social jollification" undoubtedly serves to promote communal bonding and thus helps forge a more cohesive social structure within the community. And, too, the attention that sectarian religious groups pay to the materials they ingest represents an almost extreme concern with boundary maintenance. That is, the conceptions of purity that dictate what foods can and cannot be ingested often symbolize a community's concern to take on identifiable characteristics that help them protect social boundaries vis-á-vis the outside world.[22] The ingestion of wine raises interesting points in relation to many sectarian groups' concern with moral purity. The exhilaration and enhanced sociability that are often produced by drinking wine make this activity suitable as a vehicle for symbolically breaking away from the structures of "normal" psychological and social reality. It potentially serves as both a means of incorporating persons into a new community and of inducting them into a felt sense of a nonvisible spiritual reality. Yet, the very antinomian effects of wine drinking also make it potentially dangerous to the maintenance of a group's emerging internal structures of authority.

The strict commitment to moral perfection so central to almost all of America's nineteenth-century religious sects made the consumption of alcohol problematic at best, and often an unambiguous act of moral degradation. This was especially true of those sectarian groups whose members were of largely Anglo-Saxon heritage (whether recent immigrants or settled New Englanders). Thus, for example, although there is reason to believe that Ann Lee drank large—perhaps excessive— amounts of wine before her death in 1784, the Shaker communes that she founded never produced wine and discouraged its use among Shakers.[23] Their ascetic piety demanded that they vigilantly suppress their natural tendencies to seek out sensual pleasure. Besides abstinence from alcohol, celibacy was part of the disciple's call to a life free from worldly vices. This same ascetic piety dominated the members of John Humphrey

Noyes's Christian commune in Oneida, New York. They, too, were called upon to express a Christian love that disciplined earthly appetites in the name of moral perfection. Although their sexual mores allowed for the fascinating institution of "complex marriage," in which every man was regarded as the husband of every woman and visa-versa, the use of alcohol among members was strongly suppressed. The moral, social, and ideological boundaries that distinguished these two communal sects required a self-conscious discipline that outwardly and inwardly eschewed the pleasures of the physical world.

As we saw in chapter 2, however, several equally strict nineteenth-century sects found wine to be a symbol of their communal ties. The Amana colonies and the Harmony Society are both examples of sectarian communities whose cohesiveness was greatly strengthened by the ceremonious sharing of wine. In each of these sectarian groups the commitment to a "separate" religious community was continuously rekindled through the interpersonal relationships fostered by the communal production and enjoyment of their own wines.

A far more interesting instance of the role wine can play in the dynamics of sectarian religion is to be found in the early history of the Mormons, or the Church of Jesus Christ of Latter-day Saints. The Latter-day Saints emerged in the 1820s in Palmyra, New York, when Joseph Smith was visited by God and Jesus, who commissioned him to set himself apart from rival denominations and to prepare himself to become a seer and prophet. It was their intention that Joseph would soon gather the righteous remnant to await the return of Christ and to establish a new order of things on this earth. The doctrines that distinguished the emerging sect were based in large part upon the long-lost teachings of Jesus that had been recorded in the *Book of Mormon* and which Joseph, with the help of the Angel Moroni, found buried in a local hillside. God subsequently delivered a series of additional revelations to Joseph, which he recorded in *Doctrine and Covenants* and other texts. The highly charismatic Joseph Smith excited his growing following with an enthusiastic faith that embodied the conviction of the imminent return of Christ, the importance of moral purity, the necessity of strong communal bonds, and the potential of every believer to have an intense personal experience of the Holy Spirit. The Mormons' zealous adherence to their newly received revelations struck their contemporaries as both fanatical and heretical. Further, their early practice of polygamy attracted additional scorn and derision and thus further set them apart from the larger Protestant culture in which they emerged.

As persecution mounted, the Mormons were forced to move westward, first to Kirtland, Ohio, then to Independence, Missouri, and finally to Nauvoo, Illinois. It was during the Nauvoo years that Joseph Smith was eventually shot by a crowd of angry citizens who felt threatened by the Mormons' growing presence in their region. Brigham Young succeeded Joseph Smith as leader of the main Mormon community, and he led the Latter-day Saints to their new kingdom in Salt Lake City, Utah. The Mormons' use of wine throughout this saga provides an additional perspective on the process by which they bonded together in a communal society of "glad hearts" that possessed the internal cohesion to withstand persecution from the outside. And, just as importantly, the gradual suppression of their members' consumption of wine reveals the stages in which a central structure of authority emerged within the church and deemed its members' "glad hearts" to be potentially disruptive of institutional stability.

The *Book of Mormon* fully sanctions the use of wine both as a natural pleasure provided by God and as a sacramental substance. For example, in one passage Jesus commanded his North American followers, the Nephites, to "take of the wine of the cup and drink of it" in honor of their Lord (III Nephi 18:8). In this respect the Latter-day Saints are in full continuity with the Judeo-Christian tradition in which wine was a form of libation used in early Israelite worship to God and in which wine symbolizes the presence of Christ in the principal sacrament of the Christian faith. The subsequent revelations given specifically to Mormons concerning the use of wine are quite interesting in that they serve to qualify the bold endorsement of wine drinking in the *Book of Mormon*. For example, on one occasion, Joseph Smith was upset that he had run out of wine with which to conduct the church's sacraments. A heavenly messenger met him as he set about in search of a new supply of wine and assured him that he need not be so concerned. The *Doctrine and Covenants* records that the Prophet was instructed to listen to the words of Jesus Christ that instructed him as follows: "For, behold, I say unto you, that it mattereth not what ye shall eat or what ye shall drink when ye partake of the sacrament, if it so be that ye do it with an eye single to my glory."[24] Joseph was at this time also worried that some of his enemies might try to poison his wine. It was thus a relief to learn from Jesus that "[w]herefore, a commandment I give unto you, that you shall not purchase wine neither strong drink of your enemies. Wherefore, you shall partake of none except it is made new among you."[25] He immediately added that "[b]ehold, this is wisdom in me; wherefore, marvel not, for the hour cometh that I will drink of the fruit of the vine with you on the earth and with Moroni, whom I have sent unto you to reveal the Book of Mormon, containing the fulness of my everlasting gospel."[26]

As the Mormons moved to Kirtland, the use of wine continued. It was used to provide "social jollification" and, at least on occasions, as a means of performing the church's principal sacrament. However, the Mormons found in Kirtland a sizable number of the local citizenry who were banding together to support temperance in the region and to try to shut down the local distilleries that fed the region with cheap whiskey. It was in this milieu that Joseph received the revelation that is commonly referred to as the Word of Wisdom. In February of 1833 it was revealed to him "that inasmuch as any man drinketh wine or strong drink among you, behold it is not good, neither meet in the sight of your Father, only in assembling yourselves together to offer up your sacraments before him. And, behold, this should be wine, yea, pure wine of the grape of the vine, of your own make."[27] With this revelation, the Mormons were officially on record as in support of the temperance cause. A key phrase included in this revelation, however, was that its advice was offered "not by commandment or constraint." Joseph Smith and his contemporaries did not interpret the Word of Wisdom as a strict demand for total abstinence as contemporary Mormons do (on September 9, 1951, in a general conference session it was decided that the true intent of the Word of Wisdom was to support total abstinence from alcohol). Thus, on the occasion of a double wedding in 1836, the Mormon Prophet recorded in his journal: "We then partook of some refreshments, and our hearts were made glad with the fruit of the vine. This is according to the pattern set by our Savior Himself, and we feel disposed to patronize all the institutions of Heaven."[28] At another marriage the Prophet was presented with "three servers of glasses filled with wine, to bless." He recorded that "it fell to my lot to attend to this duty which I cheerfully discharged. It was then passed round in order, then the cake in the same order; suffice it to say, our hearts were made glad while partaking of the bounty of earth, which was presented, until we had taken our fill; and joy filled every bosom."[29] On yet another occasion, Smith's records indicate that he took his mother and Aunt Clarissa in a carriage to nearby Painesville, Ohio, where they "produced a bottle of wine, broke bread, ate and drank, and parted after the ancient order with the blessing of God."[30]

LaMar Petersen has contended that in the Kirtland, Independence, and Nauvoo years, the Mormons drank wine to excess. Caution must be exercised in assessing Petersen's allegations. An ex-Mormon, Petersen's account undoubtedly vents personal resentments. Yet, Petersen maintains that even though Joseph Smith was seldom seen intoxicated in public, he drank quite intemperately both in his own home and in the barroom in the back of his store in Nauvoo.[31] Whether this charge concerning Jo-

Painting of the nineteenth-century village of Nauvoo where, according to accounts, the Latter-day Saints used wine for community celebrations. Reprinted by permission of Nauvoo Restoration Incorporated.

seph Smith's penchant for excessive drinking is true or not, Petersen is correct that the historical record indicates that a good many Mormons enjoyed wine during the faith's early years. In a world that otherwise presented them with much hard work, scarce resources, and bitter persecution, wine served to bring the early Mormon community together for conversation and merriment. Petersen quotes a Mormon who recounts that they "were in the habit of having what they called feasts. . . . They generally had two pails of wine. It was called a feast. We had a tincup and when the audience was convened and a speech made then with a cup in each pail they passed around the pails, the women on one side of the house and the men on the other, and we had as much wine as we wanted. Then we had a hymn and sometimes prayer. Then the wine would be passed around again, and then we would have cakes and wine. . . . After the cakes and wine had been passed it was the season then to speak with tongues and I spoke with the rest."[32]

These Mormon feasts performed a vital role in providing new members with a personal experience of religious ecstasy. For thousands of years wine has accompanied the worship or cultus of numerous religious traditions and helped to stimulate the altered mood or state of consciousness in which persons are more likely to feel the inflow of some energizing spiritual force. It is apparent from the account above that wine fostered new recruits' sense of living on the boundary between this world and a dawning new spiritual order. And, in this way, the religious enthusiasm so central to the early stages in the formation of a new religious sect was transmitted to the widening group of converts.

In addition to its role in inducing religious euphoria, wine was also an important means by which Mormons forged a sense of warmth and intimacy within the gathered flock. One of Joseph Smith's bodyguards, Oliver Huntington, recorded in his journal an associate's version of a typical Mormon outdoor sacrament meeting in 1838: "The people came together in the morning without their breakfast to the bowery on the Public Square where there was prepared a plenty of good bread and a barrel of wine. The bread and wine was blessed, every person ate bread and drank wine as they wanted all day, when they wanted. They sat and talked and walked and conversed upon heavenly and spiritual things as they felt like."[33] Wine and dancing parties were common in the early years, especially at the Masonic hall built in Nauvoo. One Mormon's diary recounts that a week before the dedication of the Nauvoo temple, a party erupted spontaneously even as the final carpentry and painting work was being done: "It was voted that Bro. Angel go and inform the Trustees that the hands were ready to drink the Barrell of Wine which had been reserved for them." A few nights later a group of workers and their wives met in the attic and "had a feast of cakes, pies, wine &c, where we enjoyed ourselves with prayer, preaching, administering for healing, blessing children, and music and Dancing until near Midnight."[34] And although such indulgence would be anathema to modern Mormons, it was an integral part of the communal life of the fledgling faith.

After the death of the Prophet, Brigham Young led the majority of the Saints to Salt Lake City, where hard economic times continued. In order to enhance their economic self-sufficiency, Young sent some Mormon colonists from Salt Lake to a region in southern Utah known as Dixie, where they were directed to raise cotton, sugar, grapes, and other "useful articles." Young appointed an experienced wine maker from Germany, John Naegle, to direct the Dixie wine industry and saw to it that vines of the Mission grape, a wine press, and a brandy distillery were brought from California. Over the next thirty years, several thousand gallons were manufactured to be used as medicine, as sacramental wine, and to be sold to non-Mormons as a source of additional revenue. The new Prophet advised, "First, by lightly pressing, make a white wine. Then give a heavier pressing and make a colored wine. Then barrel up this wine, and if my counsel is taken, this wine will not be drunk here, but will be exported, and thus increase the fund."[35] Unfortunately, the Dixie Mormons were sufficiently far away from Young that they did not heed his advice too strictly, and they ended up consuming a great deal of their own wine. In 1900, three years after wine was last used in the sacrament, church officials ordered the Dixie wine operation to be discontinued.[36] From that time on, total abstinence became the official means of adhering to the Word of Wisdom.

It cannot be known for certain just why the Latter-day Saints gradually adopted their total ban upon alcoholic beverages. Several factors played a role, and it is nearly impossible now to reconstruct precisely what significance to assign each of them. First and foremost would seem to be the church's millennial expectancy and the accompanying desire of the Saints to be morally pure before their Lord. The disciplining of the mind and body through abstinence is obviously an important expression of this religious commitment. As was noted earlier about evangelical faiths generally, alcohol tends to release the wrong emotions or to prevent the emotions from being properly centered on what ought to be their true object. A second factor was undoubtedly that of obtaining economic self-sufficiency by no longer importing costly alcoholic beverages or by sacrificing the efficiency of their work force.[37] A third reason pertains to the fact that by this point in their development, it became important for Mormons to define clearly the notion of a separate Mormon culture. That is, it seems that the Mormons gradually adopted strategies that would insist upon their distinctiveness and that would accentuate what they did not have in common with other Americans. Having already forged a great deal of internal cohesion, it was important for them to adopt rules of conduct that would establish clear boundaries between themselves and those on the "outside" of their theocratic community.[38] As a corollary to this important point, it would also seem that the emotional contagion and inner ecstasy associated with past Mormon use of wine was no longer functional for their community. At some point, wine and its attendant blurring of normal lines of decorum and established authority no longer served to help draw individuals away from their past identities and into a new order. Instead, the uncontrolled drinking of wine became a potential threat to the newly established internal order of the faith. As the anthropologist Victor Turner has pointed out, the "spontaneous communitas" whereby religions are originally imbued with a sense of ecstasy and communal bonding will inevitably become routinized and stripped of its spontaneous or order-threatening character.[39] Wine, as we have seen, is capable of encouraging a certain "variation in ideas" and a sense of spontaneous venturing beyond established opinions and hence over time often becomes inconsistent with the ongoing preservation of a closed theological canon.

It is of historical interest that five years after the Mormons' exodus from Nauvoo, Etienne Cabet moved his communistic sect, the Icarians, into the empty Mormon homes. The Icarians believed in a brand of secular humanism that they thought constituted "real Christianity" because it put the moral teachings of Jesus—but not religious teachings about Jesus's divine nature—into daily practice. Wine was an important beverage in this short-lived community, and one of its members, Emile Baxter, started a winery that is still in operation.

Just as with denominations, however, the various sectarian religious groups that have emerged in American religious history have had quite different attitudes toward the consumption of alcohol. Although we have seen that many of the German communal religions that flourished in the nineteenth century enthusiastically endorsed wine consumption, most American sectarian groups have followed the path of the later Mormon leaders and have offered stern admonitions against all alcohol consumption. In fact, all five of the largest native-American religious groups have issued quite specific teachings about health and moral purity that emphasize abstinence. The Seventh-Day Adventists, Jehovah's Witnesses, Christian Scientists, and various Pentecostal churches (e.g., Assemblies of God) share the Church of Jesus Christ of Latter-day Saints' opposition to the drinking of alcohol. With the possible exception of Christian Science, which comes from a very different theological tradition, the other four sizable sectarian groups are characteristically "ascetic" in their orientation to religion. Each emphasizes the need for moral and personal purity. Each expects the imminent return of Christ to judge humanity. Each consequently expects intense commitment among its members to prepare themselves for this judgment. And each would agree with the nineteenth-century revivalist preacher William Miller, who warned his followers that those who imbibed would be "wholly unprepared" for the Second Coming of Christ.[40] The refusal to embrace wine drinking, even for the purpose of religious services, is tied part and parcel with these sectarian groups' strong belief in the apostasy not only of secular American culture but of the "fashionable" churches as well. Thus, even though wine has enabled many smaller sectarian religious groups to promote communal spirit, the prohibition of wine has enabled a good many other sectarian groups to define their organization's boundaries and their members' lifestyles in ways that clearly demarcate them from those whom they believe are "wholly unprepared" to be counted among the righteous remnant.

Wine in the Life of Two "Cult" Communities

The term cult is typically used to refer to a group whose theological outlook varies dramatically from the culture's dominant religious institutions. Whereas the major denominations and sects in the United States all espouse some connection with the Judeo-Christian tradition, what we call cults are religious groups whose religious interests lie outside this tradition. In some cases a small Christian or Jewish group can be considered a cult if it emphasizes certain doctrines or lifestyle codes to the point that mainstream culture finds their religiosity to be bizarre or fanatic. The key factor in appending the label of cult to a religious group, however, is simply that its religious interests and practices are quite remote from the more socially established religious organizations. Such, for example, was clearly the case with the "Brotherhood of the New Life" community founded by the famed spiritualist medium, Thomas Lake Harris. Harris, whom the noted American philosopher and psychologist William James referred to as the "best known American mystic" in his *The Varieties of Religious Experience,* formed a religious

Thomas Lake Harris, nineteenth-century mystic and producer of wines containing a "divine aura." Reprinted by permission of Harris-Oliphant Papers, Columbia University Libraries in the City of New York.

sect that bears many resemblances to what is today known as "New Age" religion.[41] Thomas Lake Harris was an English-born minister in the liberal Universalist Church until his commitment to Swedenborgian and spiritualist theological beliefs prompted him to organize a new religious group committed to providing every individual with a personal experience of "the Divinity within." Harris was convinced that "to believe in God is but to believe that the spirit which we feel flowing into ourselves flows from an Infinite Existing Source."[42] A great deal of his career was spent in the attempt to understand the mystical states of consciousness that enable persons to open themselves up to spiritual influences never perceived by our normal waking state of consciousness.[43] The spiritualism he advocated did entail making contact with the souls of departed human beings, but it did not entail all the gaudy showmanship so often associated with spiritualist seances. The true purpose of spiritualism, he proclaimed, was to learn to be receptive to the "spirit of Christ, which descends to be immanent in the heart."[44]

As a mystic, Harris was adept at entering into entranced states of consciousness in which he claimed that disembodied spirits would use him as a medium through which to deliver sermons and sundry moral or religious advice. He began to gather a following eager to become a part of this charismatic dispensation from the spirit world, and he founded a series of colonies for the Brotherhood of the New Life in Mountain Cove, West Virginia, in Wassaic, New York, in Amenia, New York, in Brocton, New York, and finally in Santa Rosa, California. In each of the Wassaic, Amenia, and Brocton locations, Harris set his disciples to the task of growing grapes and producing wines. As Harris put it, the major commercial activity of the Brotherhood of the New Life was to be "the manufacture and sale of pure, native wine, made especially for medicinal purposes."[45] With the financial backing of his followers' savings, including the jewels of fellow occultist Lady Maria Oliphant and her son, Laurence Oliphant, a British author and member of Parliament, Harris built enormous wineries. For example, the Brocton winery was set up to manufacture about fifteen thousand gallons annually and included a massive wine cellar to house at least this much; the colony in California was even more extensive and could produce as much as twenty thousand gallons per year.

The real importance of wine for the Brotherhood of the New Life was, however, not commercial. For Harris, wine was a sacramental substance that could directly communicate divine spirit to those who properly consumed it. The Brotherhood's theology rested squarely on the premise that we all have the inward capacity to open up to, and avail ourselves of, an "influx of divine Breath." Harris, in conjunction with his angelic tutors on the other side, explained to his followers that God is continuously infusing a consecrating, revitalizing energy into the natural order. The secret of life is to learn to commune with and be filled by this infusing spiritual presence. It was in this connection that wines held such a vital place in the Brotherhood faith. Harris's mystic vision revealed to him that his wines had divine and miraculous powers. Harris claimed that his wines released the "finer electro-vinous spirit" from the grape and that they were "infused with the divine aura, potentialized in the joy spirit."[46] The very act of drinking Brotherhood wines opened individuals to an inflow of the creative breath of God. Because Brotherhood wines were infused with the divine aura, it was claimed that they could not produce alcoholic intoxication or in any way harm those who consumed them. A contemporary noted that the Brotherhood sold these wines "for the refreshment of passing travelers": "It was not merely material food and drink that were given out to them by those consecrated hands; for every glass of wine and helping of solid food to each passing traveler carried with it into the world through him an incipient ability to organic openness to the pure Breath of God."[47]

As mentioned earlier, Harris eventually moved his community from Brocton, New York, to just north of Santa Rosa, California, where once again the Brotherhood set about making divine wines. During these years Harris apparently began to give new emphasis to his doctrines concerning the sexual nature of God. The practical consequence of this conception of God was the teaching that every man and woman has a celestial counterpart. Harris taught that it is part of our spiritual duty to seek out our celestial counterparts and join with them both in sexual union and in eternal marriage. We will never know just what role wine played in Harris's pursuit of celestial sexual union, but his numerous efforts to find his one, true celestial counterpart led to a series of scandals. By the early 1890s rumors and lawsuits surfaced charging Harris with wielding dictatorial power over his disciples, appropriating their personal wealth for his private use, and encouraging illicit sexual relations among colony members. Amidst these charges he abruptly left the country for England, only to return to the United States in his last years in relative obscurity. The Brotherhood winery Harris founded at Brocton was purchased by a pair of wine merchants from New York and, although subsequently merged with another winery in Washingtonville, is currently the oldest active winery in the United States.[48] Somewhat ironically, the winery survived Prohibition by producing altar wines for mainstream Protestant and Catholic churches.

A second religious group under the broad designation of "cult" also merits attention for its extraordinary association of wine with the pursuit of an expanded spiritual consciousness. The group, known as Summum, is perhaps best understood as belonging to recently emerging religious groups that are frequently referred to as New Age religions. The term New Age is used to categorize a host of religious groups that believe that health, spiritual fulfillment, and even economic well-being can be had if we learn to find inner harmony with some higher metaphysical reality. Much of what is today called New Age religion is little more than the resurfacing of interests that appeared in the nineteenth century in such metaphysical movements as Swedenborgianism, mesmerism, Theosophy, and the kind of spiritualism advocated by Thomas Lake Harris. Thus such patently New Age interests as trance channeling (receiving messages from the spirit world while in a special trance state), crystal healing, reincarnation, and communication with intelligent extraterrestrial life are not so much new religious interests as a renewed enthusiasm that Americans have historically shared for exploring uncharted spiritual territories. Adherents of these groups typically abhor alcoholic intoxication as a harmful pollution of body, mind, and spirit. Yet, of all forms of alcohol, wine in moderation is fairly common among New Age enthusiasts. Its light and "natural" properties imbue it with a sacramental sense that makes it appropriate both for the enhancement of one's joy for living or for communal ceremonies. All of this is expressed in Summum's fascination for the spiritual potentials to be developed through the proper use of wine.

Label from the "Nectar Publication" wines produced by Summum. Reproduced by permission of Summum.

Summum® Nectar Publication of Transformation White Wine

Produced and Bottled by Summum®, Salt Lake City, Utah
Net contents 750 ML   Alcohol 13% by Volume

Mr. Claude Nowell was an elder in the Mormon Church and living in Salt Lake City when, in 1974, he began to notice a "ringing" in his ears while sitting in his den and relaxing after work.[49] This intense but peaceful ringing returned each day during his daily relaxation period. About one year later, Mr. Nowell turned his attention away from all outside noise and directed it to the sound within his mind. He reports that when he opened his eyes he was standing next to an enormous pyramid and surrounded by a strange-looking group of individuals who looked similar to humans, yet had light blue skin and wore no clothes. These individuals led him to a large crystal shaft that emanated an invisible energy or wisdom toward him, directly transmitting an entire set of "higher truths" to the recesses of his consciousness. Mr. Nowell explains that this was not a case of "channeling"—whereby a disembodied spirit delivers a complete message to an entranced human—rather, the crystal emanated concepts to his psyche, but he had to work out an understanding or articulation of the concepts on his own.

Since that first encounter in 1975, Claude Nowell has visited with these extraterrestrial beings more than fifty times. These beings, whom he refers to as Summa Individuals, have identified themselves as souls who evolved out of ancient Atlantis and have mastered the secrets of the universe (which are recorded in and can be communicated by their crystals). The Summa Individuals are dedicated to working with all people

Label from the "Nectar Publication" wines produced by Summum. Reproduced by permission of Summum.

who are ready to subordinate their human egos and take up the labor of spiritual evolution. Claude Nowell has worked with the Summa Individuals for over fifteen years, and his continued spiritual growth is reflected in the fact that he now goes by the name of Summum Bonum Amen Ra.

Summum Bonum Amen Ra has constructed what might be called a New Age religious center outside of Salt Lake City to assist others in their spiritual ascension. Much of the spiritual path advocated by Summum has to do with meditation exercises aimed at expanding personal consciousness and with studying the teachings that come down from ancient Atlantis and ancient Egypt through the Summa Individuals.[50] A major teaching concerns the "rediscovery" of the unique liquids used by ancient religious peoples to convey spiritual power and information to those who ingest them. Summum publications refer to the soma beverage used to bring enlightenment to ancient Hindu sages and to the "nectars of the gods" referred to in the hieroglyphs of ancient Egypt:

> These liquids, the Nectar Publications, old messengers of communication, were tools of the Initiates. Since then, thousands of years have passed, and in 1975 evolved Atlantean Initiates [the Summa Individuals] re-established Summum, a society whose many purposes was to begin recreation of those same nectars. Referred to as publications because of the information they contain, these nectars are provided by the Summum for the benefit of this planet and the inhabitancy thereof.[51]

To make these wines, usually referred to as "nectar publications," Nowell built a three-story pyramid that rests on large quartz-crystals and is precisely aligned on a north-south axis. Within this pyramid—the womb of creation as Summum refers to it—several large stainless steel vats are used to make consciousness-expanding wine. At astrologically precise times, juices and other "essences of nature" are placed in the vats along with one teaspoon of powdered crystal rock per every fifteen hundred gallons. For a period of seventy-seven days, Summum initiates use meditation techniques designed to project spiritual energies and information into the fermenting "nectars." They believe that the powdered crystal suspended with the liquid acts as a receptor and capacitor of their meditationally projected energies. The powdered crystal is then able to transfer these energies to the subatomic particles in the liquid.

The nectars are then bottled and stored in the pyramid, intensifying the energy and information that are contained within them. Although the state of Utah prohibits the sale of wine except through licensed state liquor stores, Summum accepts donations in return for bottles from one of seven different nectars that they have produced to date (Summum plans eventually to produce twenty-seven nectars in all). As a person uses a small amount of nectar prior to meditation, his or her life force energy dissolves the crystals in the body, releasing the resonations or energies into the alcohol. The alcohol then carries the resonations across the blood brain barrier where the information is released and gradually assimilated into the person's consciousness. It is recommended that new initiates use small amounts of the nectar twice daily, morning and evening, followed by meditation, in order to transform their consciousness to an ascended level at which the Summum Bonum—the Supreme Good— permeates their very being.

Strangely enough, a "cult," such as Summum, a "sect," such as the Church of Jesus of Latter-day Saints, and a "denomination," such as Episcopalians or Conservative Judaism, have all found wine to perform functions vital to their respective religious identities. It is quite possible that the labels denomination, sect, and cult prove too cumbersome to be of real value and perhaps perpetuate the very kind of pejorative classifying of religious groups that they were initially intended to eliminate. In fact, the word "sect" has the larger meaning of signifying any and all religious groups. And, to be sure, every religious group shares the double task of providing its members both with an experience of a higher spiritual reality and with a felt sense of affiliation with a cohesive religious tradition or community. Wine, it seems, has frequently played an important role in this shared "sectarian experience." The use—or nonuse—of wine reveals much about a group's theological disposition toward ritually structured religious experience. And, perhaps even more clearly, a religious group's use—or nonuse—of wine reveals much about the kinds of interpersonal relationships that will best enable members to sustain their identification with that religious community. In general, the further a group is from America's social and/or theological "establishment," the more likely the group is to take a dramatic stand for or against wine as a symbolic statement of its distinctive sense of spirituality and its distinctive vision of religious community. Wine, then, provides a fascinating perspective on the American sectarian experience and accentuates the continuing creativity of American culture in giving rise to new forms of religious enthusiasm.

CHAPTER 4

The Grapes of Wrath
PROHIBITION

Not every American religious group shared George Husmann's jubilant vision of America developing into a happy wineland where persons might daily enjoy the "purest and most wholesome of all stimulants." Throughout the nineteenth century a good many religious voices began to speak out against what they considered a vice that threatened the realization of the Kingdom of God on earth. This vice was first identified to be the intemperate use of distilled spirits. Yet, as the century progressed, so, too, did views concerning the scope of this vice until it was understood to include the consumption of any alcohol whatsoever. The shift from the advocacy of temperance to the insistence upon a total prohibition of alcohol implicated American religion in a major social and cultural drama. Numerous religious individuals and organizations took the lead in a movement that, by attacking persons' lifestyles and understandings of happiness or fulfillment, was fraught with elements of class hatred, ethnic prejudice, and general fear of America's increasing pluralism. Many religious organizations found themselves in the paradoxical situation of denouncing a substance that had for centuries been central to both Jewish and Christian worship. The changing attitudes of American religious groups toward wine reflect tensions in a religious system confused as to how it might best impose order upon, or even preserve itself within, an ever more diverse society.

The Alcoholic Republic

Contemporary Americans generally find the Prohibition movement incomprehensible and dismiss it as a misdirected outburst of moral zeal. It becomes more comprehensible, however, when we reconstruct the social and cultural contexts that made the consumption of alcohol so problematic to established religious groups in the nineteenth and early twentieth centuries. The first European settlers in America thought of alcohol as a necessary part of wholesome living. Drinking water was in short supply in an era that lacked power drilling equipment to dig deep wells and underground piping to bring water to homes in growing villages and cities. Water was also a health hazard owing to the frequency of diseases and ailments that were transmitted through infected water supplies. By contrast, beverages such as cider, beer, rum, whiskey, and wine were safer for human consumption. They were thought to be capable of warming the body and to have numerous medicinal purposes. A drink kept off fevers and chills, aided digestion, and raised persons' spirits. And, in an age lacking today's prepackaged pain relievers, alcoholic beverages served as a general tonic that enabled persons to cope better with their various physical ailments.

Beginning with the Pilgrims at the Plymouth Colony, alcohol was a staple in the early American diet. In fact, when the *Mayflower* arrived off the coast of Massachusetts, the beer supply was already nearly consumed.[1] A dramatic struggle over the remaining supply of beer ensued between the desperate colonists and the sailors aboard the *Mayflower*. The esteemed governor and historian of the Plymouth Colony, William Bradford, recorded that the settlers "were hasted ashore and made to drink water" so that "the seamen might have the more beer." The ship captain finally relented in the face of the settlers' misery and sent word that there would be "beer for them that had need for it," even if his crew would have to go without on their return voyage. Yet, when the *Mayflower* set sail on its return voyage, the full impact of the alcohol shortage set in. Necessity proved the mother of fermentation, and the colonists promptly set about the task of insuring a steady local supply. Hence, local beer and local wine were probably already present to give thanks at a fall celebration.

Future settlements came better prepared. Thus, for example, when the *Arbella* set sail for Boston in 1630 with a load of Puritans heading for religious freedom in the New World, it carried ten thousand gallons of wine and three times more beer than water.[2] Colonial entrepreneurs were quick to seize an opportunity and made sure that demand was matched by supply. Rum trade with the West Indies, local efforts at brewing and wine making, and newly constructed American distilleries soon turned open the spigot of alcohol flow in the colonies. The nineteenth-century minister and temperance historian Daniel Dorchester records that by 1792 there were 2,579 distilleries operating in the United States; by 1810, there were 14,191.[3]

Nearly every colonial town had one or more taverns to dispense this immense supply of God's good creature. Taverns were a vital part of community life in this era and were often among the first buildings erected in any new village.[4] They provided a retail outlet for liquor, food, and lodging for travelers, and one of the few forums for informal gatherings where one might discuss political and religious issues. Colonial taverns were thus more than just drinking establishments; they filled a variety of practical social needs and were in many ways the center of village culture. Popular culture, of course, did not always perfectly mirror the values and lifestyles that the clergy espoused from the pulpit. For example, Reverend Dorchester, who despised these dens of infidelity, tried to awaken his readers to the dangers of this setting in which "the great fireplaces, with abundant fuel, huge backlogs and loggerhead, were kept at white heat" while sundry drinks "were dispensed to the motley assembly, who came together to hear the news, gossip and talk politics."[5]

By any account, alcohol was prevalent and pervasive in colonial America. This was especially true at funerals, ordinations, military maneuvers of any sort, and political campaigning or elections. Drinking at funerals frequently took on gargantuan proportions. And, especially among the upper classes, funerals were often an occasion when one might splurge and buy expensive imported wine to honor the memory of the deceased. Dorchester came upon records that testify to the lavish nature of these funerals:

> [I]n 1678, at the funeral of Mrs. Mary Norton, widow of the celebrated John Norton, one of the ministers of the First Church in Boston, fifty-one gallons and a half of the best Malaga wine were consumed by the "mourners"; in 1685, at the funeral of Rev. Thomas Cobbett, minister of Ipsich, there were consumed one barrel of wine and two barrels of cider, and "as it was cold," there were "some spice and ginger for the cider." You may easily judge of the drunkenness and riot on occasions less solemn than the funerals of old and beloved ministers.[6]

The ordination of a minister was apparently one of these "less solemn" occasions. In his *The Life and Times of the Late Demon Rum*, J. C. Furnas relates how the installation of Rev. John Cornell as minister of the local Presbyterian congregation turned into a drinkfest typical of the era's ordination ceremonies. The tavern ledger indicates that the members of the local presbytery gathered for the event owed a sizable sum for "dinner, feed for their horses, four large bowls of punch, a pit of brandy, one 'go' of grog, two bottles of wine, and three and a half bottles of beer."[7] The famed nineteenth-century Presbyterian minister Lyman Beecher was so appalled by the excessive drinking at ministers'

Lyman Beecher, prototypical
nineteenth-century Protestant
temperance preacher.

ordination ceremonies that he became one of the first to harness the
forces of evangelical Protestantism to the growing call for temperance.[8]

Alcohol was also a mainstay in the various colonial militia organizations. Pre-Revolutionary militia drills were little more than ornate ex-
cuses for drinking hysterics. During the Revolution, a daily liquor ration (usually of whiskey since the imported molasses for rum was hard
to come by) was used as a form of partial compensation and to boost
morale. And, finally, the "treating" of voters to a plenteous supply of
spirits was a major part of American political campaigning well into
the nineteenth century. It was considered important that a candidate
demonstrate generosity and hospitality by inviting voters to help themselves to as much drink as they could handle. When wooing voters of
the upper class, a candidate would typically offer imported wines. But
when electioneering among the middle and working classes, it was important to demonstrate patriotism and disdain for imported goods by
dispensing rye whiskey or cider. It was not so much the offer of free
booze as it was the symbolic gesture of fraternizing that made "treating" important to American politics. The common man was typically
suspicious of the upper classes. By sharing a drink, candidates demonstrated their ties with the ordinary folk and their commitment to egalitar-
ian principles. The symbolic "leveling" whereby drinking forged bonds between politicians and the citizenry was also present in relations between

the clergy and those they hoped to lure into being parishioners. One cir-
cuit-riding minister in the Trans-Appalachian West was confronted by
a man who frankly stated that "if I did not drink with him, I was no
friend of his, or his family, and he would never hear me preach again."[9]

The Religious Call to Temperance

It was within this sociocultural context that the first voices for temperance and prohibition began to speak out. The most important of these
early calls for temperance came from the respected physician, Dr. Benjamin Rush. Dr. Rush was one of the leading professionals in the Revolutionary era. He was, in fact, a signer of the Declaration of Independence and enjoyed the reputation of being the foremost physician in
the early Republic. Rush began to speak out against the almost universal assumption that alcohol was beneficial in almost any form or any
amount. His *An Inquiry into the Effects of Ardent Spirits on the Human
Mind and Body* (1784) declared that, far from being a general tonic or pana-
cea, alcohol more frequently destroys the body and often leads directly to
death. He also directed attention to the progressive debilitation wrought
by alcohol addiction and championed the view that alcoholism is a disease
that takes control of individuals and compels them to life-destroying behaviors that are beyond their ability to control.

Rush was not advocating total abstinence and probably never thought
of himself as a visionary behind any widespread movement such as was
to emerge just a few years after his death. Yet he did speak out with a
sense of urgency. He perceived the pervasive use of hard liquor to be a
threat to persons' health. Equally on his mind were the social consequences of alcohol addiction and the threat they posed to the fledgling
nation he had worked so hard to bring into existence. Rush was convinced that the debilitating nature of alcohol led inevitably to crime,
squandering of family income, breakdown of the family unit, and moral
degradation. To prevent this gradual corruption of American society,
Rush proposed that stiffer penalties be placed upon public drunkenness, that sanitariums be constructed for alcoholics, and that taverns be
more carefully controlled and more heavily taxed by the government.
Thus, although he was not calling for a total prohibition of alcohol,
Rush signaled the shift in Americans' attitudes toward curbing the
nation's prodigious drinking habits.

The zeal behind the growing temperance movement clearly came
from the revivalistic or evangelical religion that dominated American
culture throughout the nineteenth century.[10] The "Second Great Awak-

ening" that flowered during the 1820s and 1830s converted thousands of Americans to evangelical Protestant faith and had a pronounced effect upon the nation's sense of moral righteousness. The revivalists' call to renounce one's sins and accept Jesus as one's personal Savior was accompanied by an exhortation to moral purity. The period's preachers also intensified expectations of the imminent return of Christ in ways that encouraged individuals to be concerned with the gradual perfection of their own lives and others' lives in order that Christ would find them morally pure and deserving of salvation. Because of America's separation of church and state, Protestantism did not seek to effect its program for the total renovation of human society through governmental agencies. Instead, American Protestantism relied upon what is known as "voluntaryism" whereby born-again persons joined volunteer organizations dedicated to the moral improvement of individuals and the larger social order. Various bible societies, groups promoting educational reform, and the abolition movement are all examples of Protestant piety directing its concern for moral perfectionism into the larger culture. So, too, was the proliferation of temperance societies.

Rorabaugh has noted that revivalist religion and temperance were inexorably linked. "In many localities revivals were held, church rosters bulged, and then six months or a year later temperance societies were organized."[11] Even though the sequence was not always uniform, temperance and evangelical Protestantism were responses to the same nineteenth-century social tensions. Continuing immigration, rapid urbanization, and the beginning of massive industrialization put strains on the more established citizenry, who were at somewhat of a loss as to how they might preserve their ordered way of life amidst what appeared to be chaos and disorder. Evangelical religion and temperance each sought to cope with the period's frustrations by seeking to structure, rationalize, and control emotions. This, of course, fit in well with the interests of the middle and upper classes, who viewed with favor the developing industrial climate that required worker efficiency, self-discipline, and orderly conduct. The intemperate use of alcohol, especially by immigrants, was a visible reminder that a sizable segment of American society defied incorporation into Protestantism's moral and religious scheme. American Protestantism responded with an impassioned effort to impose sobriety and order upon that unruly social element. After all, drunkenness impairs humans' reason, weakens their conscience, dissipates their fear of God, and prompts them to commit vices of most every kind. By fostering ungodliness, alcohol undermined American Protestantism's official mission of saving souls and incorporating reclaimed souls into a well-regulated moral community. And although such culturally "established" denominations such as the Congregationalists, Episcopalians, and Presbyterians did not share the pietistic zeal of the more evangelical Baptists and Methodists, they were surely drawn together in a shared mission of defining the nation's religious and moral outlook. They were also drawn together by class interests as they found themselves largely dominating the upper and middle classes and increasingly separated from the political and economic agendas of non-Protestant, immigrant workers. Religious, economic, and political interests thus bonded a growing number of Protestants in a crusade to curtail the disrupting influences of those who hindered their plans to create a well-ordered Protestant nation.

At first the nineteenth-century temperance societies fought only distilled spirits. But as their ranks grew, so too did their conception of moral pollutants. Soon the phrase "all intoxicating beverages" replaced "ardent spirits" on the societies' pledge cards, and a new battle line was drawn over the wine question. Indeed, many nineteenth-century reformers had thought that wine was a godsend in that wine provided a less-intoxicating alternative to hard liquor. Thomas Jefferson had asserted as fact that "no nation is drunken where wine is cheap; and none sober, where the dearness of wine substitutes ardent spirits as the common beverage. It is, in truth, the only antidote to the bane of whiskey."[12] Dr. Benjamin Rush also made a clear distinction between wine and other alcoholic beverages, and he unambiguously advocated wine as a sanative substitute for ardent spirits. Later editions of Rush's classic work on the harmful effects of liquor included a chart entitled "A Moral and Physical Thermometer: or, a Scale of the Progress of Temperance and Intemperance." Rush's chart equated the consumption of distilled spirits with obscenity, swindling, and murder. Wine, on the other hand, was associated with the virtues of "cheerfulness, strength, and nourishment."

Even the religious-minded Charles Nordhoff, in his survey of the period's communal religious groups, points out:

> [T]hey are temperate in the use of wine or spirits, and drunkenness is unknown in all the communes, although among the Germans the use of wine and beer is universal. The American communes do not use either at all. But at Economy or Amana or Zoar the people receive either beer or wine daily, and especially in harvest-time, when they think these more wholesome than water. At Economy they have very large, substantially built wine cellars, where some excellent wine is stored.
>
> Is it not possible that the general moderation with which life is pursued in a commune, the quiet, absence of exciting or worrying cares, regularity of habit and easy work, by keeping their blood cool, decrease

Benjamin Rush's Temperance Thermometer. Reproduced with the assistance of Knox College Library. Originally published in *The Gentleman's Magazine*.

the tendency to misuse alcoholic beverages? There is no doubt that in the German communes wine and beer are used, and have been for many years, in a way which would be thought dangerous by our temperance people; but I have reason to believe without the occurrence of any case of habitual intemperance. Possibly scientific advocates of temperance may hereafter urge a more temperate and sensible pursuit of wealth and happiness, a less eager life and greater contentment, as more conducive to what we narrowly call "temperance" than all the total-abstinence pledges.[13]

Nordhoff wholly misgauged his fellow evangelical Protestants. They were not about to live a "less eager life" or go about a more "sensible pursuit of wealth." But they were gearing up to wage a campaign against those who resisted the "total-abstinence pledges," with which they hoped to reform society in ways pleasing to Christ. Evangelical Protestants, drawn from nearly all denominations but with a decided concentration of ascetic-leaning Methodists, began forming local temperance societies and circulating temperance pledges. By 1826 the American Society for the Promotion of Temperance (later to be known as the American Temperance Society) emerged as the first national temperance organization. Other such organizations, including the influential Women's Christian Temperance Union, were soon joining the cause and helping to carry the banner of sobriety. As their numbers grew, pressure increased to expand the scope of temperance to include the total prohibition of all alcohol whatsoever. Reverend Dorchester records that the "very able report on Temperance adopted by the General Conference of the Methodist Episcopal Church" in 1832 concluded that "[w]e are the more disposed to press the necessity of entire abstinence, because there seems to be no safe line of distinction between the moderate and the immoderate use of intoxicating drinks; the transition from the moderate to the immoderate use of them is almost as certain as it is insensible; indeed, it is with us a question of great moral interest, whether a man can indulge in their use at all and be considered temperate."[14]

Interestingly, the total abstinence issue came up the very next year at the National Temperance Convention held in Philadelphia in May of 1833. It was speedily voted down. Dorchester reports that the reason was that "Many of the original apostles of the temperance movement . . . were ardent advocates for the culture of the grape, urging a generous home production of pure wine as a preventive of the ravages of intemperance."[15] As Dorchester indicated, many upper-class Protestants in the East were offended that the very societies they voluntarily contributed funds to for the purpose of uplifting society's rabble were now turning the attack upon their own favorite beverage. In fact, donations

Signing the Temperance Pledge. Originally published in Daniel Dorchester, *Liquor Problem in All Ages* (1884).

to the many state and local temperance organizations fell off dramatically when many genteel supporters were made to feel uneasy about their Madeira. Wine, after all, had long been regarded as symbolic of the very substance of Christ and was used to celebrate the most sacred of Christian rituals. It had tradition and heritage behind it. Moreover, because wine is produced through spontaneous fermentation, it was considered "natural" in a way that distilled spirits were not. For these reasons, wine drinkers began to issue articulate editorials against the zealous reaches of the temperance movement. To no avail, it seems.

A National Temperance Convention was called in 1836 to debate the "wine question" at length. The convention resulted in a report that resolved "That we view with special approbation, and hail as a token for good, the formation [of increasing numbers of temperance societies] on the plan of total abstinence from all intoxicating liquor."[16] The American Society for the Promotion of Temperance issued a statement defining temperance as the moderate and proper use of things beneficial and the abstinence from things hurtful. It followed that alcoholic beverages, since they are a "poison" and thus among "the things hurtful," must be abstained from. Temperance societies began to press their new members to sign temperance pledges that included a vow of total abstinence. In this way, the "wine issue" gave rise to the term "teetotaler." Although rival accounts of the emergence of this term locate the setting in Hector, New York, Scotland, or England, it remains clear that individuals who signed temperance pledges put the initials "T.A." next to their name if they were vowing not simple temperance but total abstinence. The number of those vowing to abstain completely would thus be found by totaling the T's.

The shift from temperance to total abstinence was, in many respects, also a shift from the advocacy of a Christian virtue to the insistence upon a social taboo. Taboos invariably reflect religiocultural notions of "purity" and a group's efforts to erect boundaries that will protect its members from these impure or tainted social elements. The taboo against wine drinking was at one level intended to protect individuals against theological impurity. As was noted in chapter 3, the evangelical temperament of nineteenth-century American Protestantism clearly favored ascetic, as opposed to aesthetic, piety. Evangelicalism emphasized the importance of a conscious, willed decision to accept Jesus as one's personal savior as the critical factor in securing personal salvation. It was expected that accompanying this decision would be a willful commitment to prevailing moral codes. The life of sanctification envisioned by nineteenth-century evangelicalism required the subordination of emotions and of the pursuit of worldly pleasures. Thus, even though emotionalism was a strong element in procuring conversion experiences, evangelical piety as a whole was strongly suspicious of any and all emotions that could not be properly directed or focused in conformity with its ascetic moral outlook. Alcohol in general threatened to release the wrong emotions, or at least to prevent the emotions from being properly centered on what evangelical faith proclaimed to be their true object. No doubt a good many temperance advocates suspected a hidden danger in wine, given its long association with upper-class intellectuals, who were simultaneously prone to variant religious philosophies. Indeed, in the American context, wine was frequently understood in a way more or less consistent with Emerson's Transcendentalism. That is, it has often been claimed that wine is a material agent susceptible of receiving direct infusions or influxes of God's gracious spirit (e.g., the Missouri viniculturist Friedrich Muench's interest in Transcendentalism, Thomas Lake Harris's claim that wines are infused with the divine aura, or Summum's belief in the ability of wine to harness cosmic energies). Such views are metaphysical anathema from the perspective of ascetic evangelism, with its insistence that individuals themselves have no inner link or capacity to initiate communion with God. As both Mary Douglas and Mircea Eliade have noted, religious taboos frequently reveal fear of the unpredictable consequences resulting from

Temperance-era scene of women crusaders protesting a tavern owner's sale of wine. Originally published in Daniel Dorchester, *Liquor Problem in All Ages* (1884).

a two-way contact with divinity.[17] Wine, therefore, was destined to come under the attack of temperance advocates no matter how much this might mean ignoring scriptural sanctions for moderate wine drinking.

The shift to a call for total abstinence also had pronounced sociological dimensions. Clearly, the shift in immigration patterns at this time had at least something to do with America's Anglo-Saxon Protestants becoming so zealous about this taboo. The Irish were the largest immigrant group in the antebellum era. Those who made the journey to the United States did so largely to escape poverty in Ireland. They were, consequently, poor, ill-educated, and lived in the squalor of urban ghettos. The drinking of whiskey, gin, and malted beverages among the Irish immigrants became a symbol of their ethnic loyalty. By century's end, Germans, Poles, Italians, and Jews of every nationality were pouring into America by the millions. With the exception of Jewish immigrants, among whom drinking outside of family and religious observances was quite rare, the new immigrants were notable for their public drinking. The Protestant majority viewed these "foreigners" with disdain. Religious and ethnic prejudice fueled the fire of Protestants' moral indignation at the immigrants' lifestyles. Protestants generally perceived them to be coarse and uncivilized. The fact that even fellow Anglo-Saxon Protestants acted this same way when under the influence of "demon rum" led to the identification of alcohol as a taboo that threatened to pull down the moral integrity even of "finer" people.

Temperance-era depiction of the "serpent" wine chalice. Originally published in Daniel Dorchester, *Liquor Problem in All Ages* (1884).

Total abstinence was, in this respect, a form of boundary-setting behavior. It should not be surprising that few nineteenth-century temperance activities were really targeted at people with serious drinking problems. Temperance activists tended to dismiss hard-core drinkers as wholly beyond redemption. Instead, abstinence was something urged upon fellow members of the established middle class. The goal of temperance was to preserve the boundaries of middle-class citizenship and to protect one another from "slipping" into behaviors that might even remotely resemble the activities of the unredeemable masses now surrounding them on all sides. It would be wrong to interpret the growing prohibitionist sentiments as rooted solely in religious and ethnic prejudice. Prohibition was also very much an ideological agenda born of Christian commitment to moral sanctification, capitalistic concern with worker efficiency, moral outrage over the erosion of family stability, and patriotic defense of the need for an alert and sober citizenry. Yet, without question, the call to prohibition had within it a certain resonance to the class and ethnic tensions of a rapidly industrializing society.

To urge total abstinence upon their fellow Americans, the temperance leaders had first to surmount two final barriers. First, they had to overcome the obvious fact that the Bible endorses the moderate drinking of wine. And, secondly, they had to address and offer a new perspective on the Christian sacrament of Holy Communion, or the Lord's Supper, in which wine was nothing less than a symbol of Christ's redeeming spirit. Reverend Dorchester gave elaborate expression to the temperance advocates' inventive view that the wines available to nineteenth-century Americans bore no resemblance to those drunk in biblical times. Dorchester went to great lengths to point out differences in soil and climate that made American wines much more harmful that the "mild, non-harmful" wines that were available in Palestine during the time of Jesus.[18] Dorchester, incidentally, duplicated Dr. Benjamin Rush's "Moral and Physical Thermometer" of alcohol consumption in later editions of his own major temperance work and deliberately omitted Rush's section that equated wine with positive virtues. For Dorchester, as with the period's other temperance writers, the moderate drinker was a vexing problem that threatened to invalidate their whole line of reasoning. This embarrassment was best avoided by ignoring the moderate wine drinker as much as possible or showing that wines were not as reliably "temperate" as they might at first appear. Numerous editorialists argued that the wine available in the United States, whether native or imported, was frequently adulterated by the adding of more potent spirits. Finally, it was argued that those persons who consumed wine in moderation were morally infectious. Even if some people can drink wine with no ill effect, their bad example leads weaker persons into iniquity and vice.[19] Thus an 1835 edition of the *Temperance Recorder* explained:

> Our views with regard to pure wine are, that the Bible sanctions its moderate use—that there can be no immorality in such use, under certain circumstances; but in our present condition with the fact that pure wine is fatal to the recovery of the drunkard, because it intoxicates, often forms the appetite for stronger drinks in the temperate, and its use by the rich hinders the poor from uniting with temperance societies— that all, or nearly all the wine in this country, is a most vile compound; these are the reasons why we urge abstinence from all wine.[20]

Pressure began to mount within each denomination to end the practice of using wine in the act of Christian worship. Unfermented grape juice was for the first time widely available on a commercial basis since Thomas Welch and others were making a sizable income catering to

Dr. Thomas Welch (center) and family. Reproduced by permission of Welch's.

the nation's newfound need for nonalcoholic beverages. Thomas Welch, a Methodist minister turned dentist, was convinced that alcohol was un-acceptable in the Christian sacrament of the Lord's Supper. Having learned of Louis Pasteur's identification of the chemical process whereby yeast and grape juice interact to form wine, Welch perfected a process whereby wine juice could be boiled and filtered in a manner that removed the alcohol-producing yeast. By 1869 he produced his first bottles of "Dr. Welch's Un-fermented Wine," which he believed would serve God by providing Chris-tians with a nonalcoholic substitute for sacramental wine. His son, Charles, later observed that "[u]nfermented grape juice was born in 1869 out of a passion to serve God by helping His Church to give its communion 'the fruit of the vine,' instead of the 'cup of devils.'"[21] Charles Welch was no less a fundamentalist and temperance advocate than his father, and he eventually took over the Welch Company. Charles undertook his position with all the zeal of an impassioned missionary. He promptly launched a successful marketing and advertising campaign to bring his unfermented grape juice to the attention of an America he deemed precariously close

Welch's grape juice factory. Reproduced by permission of Welch's.

to straying from God's ways. Charles, incidentally, was a delegate to numerous Methodist conferences and was even a delegate on the worship committee that adopted grape juice, not wine, as the beverage to be used in the Methodists' observance of the Lord's Supper.

The evangelical churches, such as the Baptists, Methodists, and Disciples of Christ, already viewed the Lord's Supper more as a memorial than as a sacrament. Now, having officially pledged themselves to obliterating all personal and social vices, they began to chide their Christian brethren for not following them in the use of unfermented grape juice rather than wine in the enactment of the Lord's Supper. Many ultra-conservative Bible scholars even went so far as to argue that all scriptural references to wine had been mistranslated and that the original text had referred to simple grape juice. But the more ritually oriented church traditions, such as the Episcopalians, Lutherans, and Roman Catholics, continued to use wine in the celebration of Holy Communion and consequently found themselves under direct ecclesiastical attack.

It might be pointed out in passing that not everyone viewed the "wine question" so seriously. Oliver Wendell Holmes offered his readers a witty parody of the period's temperance fervor when he published the "slight alterations" he had to make at the last minute in verses that he had ostensibly written for a banquet, unaware that it was to be a teetotal affair:

Come! fill a fresh bumper,—for why should we go
    logwood
While the ~~nectar~~ still reddens our cups as they flow!
    decoction
Pour out the ~~rich juices~~ still bright with the sun,
        dye-stuff
Till o'er the brimmed crystal the ~~rubies~~ shall run.
  half-ripened apples
The ~~purple globed clusters~~ their life-dews have bled;
      taste   *sugar of lead*
How sweet is the ~~breath~~ of the ~~fragrance they shed!~~
    rank poisons   *wines*!!!
For summer's ~~last roses~~ lie hid in the ~~wines~~
       stable-boys smoking long-nines.
That were garnered by ~~maidens who laughed through the vines~~
  scowl   *howl*   *Scoff*   *sneer*
Then a ~~smile~~, and a ~~glass~~, and a ~~toast~~, and a ~~cheer~~,
   strychnine and whiskey, and ratsbane and beer
For all the ~~good wine, and we've some of it here~~

In cellar, in pantry, in attic, in hall,
Down, down, with the tyrant that masters us all!
~~Long live the gay servant that laughs for us all!~~[22]

The Push to Prohibition

By the second decade of the twentieth century the "total abstinence" cause gained considerable momentum. The moral thrust of Protestantism joined forces with the Progressive Movement, which sought to improve the condition of the underprivileged through political and economic reforms. As James Timberlake has argued, alcohol prohibition became a celebrated cause in the Progressive Movement because it promised to remove from commerce an article that despoils humans' reason, undermines representative government, and erodes the moral foundations of our religious and cultural heritage.[23] The Progressive Movement sought to make America more efficient and reflected an optimistic belief in the desirability of material progress; in Prohibition, Progressivist reformers combated a tangible enemy of efficiency and productivity. The Progressive Movement was out to curb the power of industrial and financial corporations; in Prohibition it was able to attack the liquor industry that was a visible symbol of the tyranny of capi-

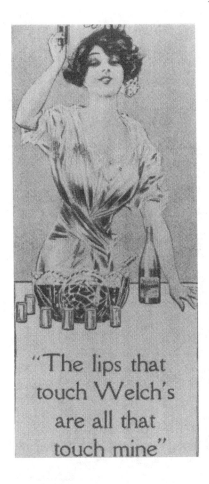

"The lips that touch Welch's are all that touch mine"

Welch's advertisement appealing to Prohibitionist sentiments. Reproduced by permission of Welch's.

talists' exploitation of the common folk's foibles. And, too, the Progressive Movement yearned to free the lower and middle classes of crime, poverty, and disease through direct legislation; through Prohibition, it found at least one identifiable target.

The combined clout of Protestant "Social Gospelers" carrying the banner of temperance and political reformers seeking to protect citizens from buying a commodity deemed not in the country's best economic and social interests created a sufficient political consensus to make possible the passage of the Volstead Act that enforced Prohibition in the United States from 1920 until it was finally repealed in 1933. What followed was perhaps the most interesting chapter in the history American viniculture.

At the outset of Prohibition, there were over seven hundred bonded wineries in the state of California alone; by the time the Eighteenth Amendment was repealed, there were only one hundred and forty.[24] Nationwide, fewer than two hundred wineries remained in operation. Those that tried to survive were forced to strip their vineyards of the finest varietals for which there was no longer a market and concentrate instead on undistinguished wines that could be made into "tonics" still legal for medicinal purposes, altar wines, and vinegar. The long-term effects of Prohibition on the American commercial wine industry are staggering. Not only did it lose the cultivated vineyards, production equipment, and trained personnel that resulted from thirteen years of enforced curtailment, but also the industry lost valuable ground in cultivating a consumer market that might at last appreciate the "most wholesome of all stimulants, good, cheap, native wine."

Ironically, although commercial wine making was devastated by the Volstead Act, wine making and wine drinking actually increased fairly substantially during Prohibition. The Volstead Act allowed for the manufacture of cider and fruit juices, as long as they were nonintoxicating. Consumers could readily buy grape juice concentrate that came with explicit instructions concerning the steps they should not take if they wanted to avoid making illegal wine at home. And, indeed, the government also issued permits for the male heads of households to make up to two hundred gallons of wine per year legally, provided that

Brother Timothy's T-shirt satirizing neoprohibitionist attacks upon wine drinking. Photo by Duane Zehr.

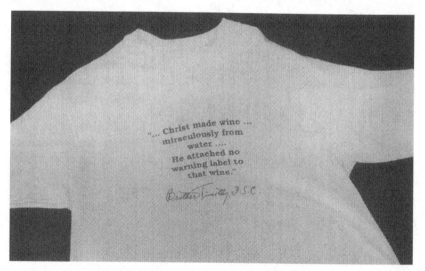

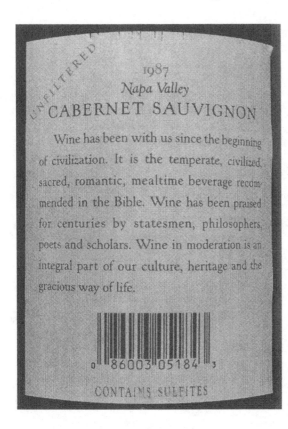

Mondavi Winery's former label seeking to remind consumers of wines religious heritage. Reproduced by permission of Robert Mondavi Winery.

this wine was not intended for commercial use. Not surprisingly, Prohibition started a seller's market for grapes, and the price of harvested grapes tripled in just a few years. It is estimated that wine consumption jumped from approximately 0.53 to 0.64 gallons per capita during Prohibition. This wine, however, was poorly made, since it was required to be neither "wholesome" nor "good," but simply cheap and intoxicating.

The Volstead Act, recognizing the "legitimate" use of wine for the purpose of religious worship, made provision for bonded wineries to sell wine "for sacramental purposes or like religious rites" to individuals such as "a rabbi, minister of the gospel, priest, or an officer duly authorized for the purpose by any church or congregation."[25] Although much of the activity inevitably spawned by this provision for "altar wines" eludes historical documentation, anecdotes abound of the formation of new religious sects with elaborate rituals requiring wine and of the inflation of membership statistics for a number of Jewish congregations in New York.

Prohibition dealt American viniculture a staggering blow. Recovery after repeal was slow and difficult. The obvious obstacles that had to be surmounted included the loss of wine-making talent, the disruption of vineyards, and the legacy of a patchwork of local laws that hampered the manufacture and interstate distribution of alcoholic beverages. Worse, however, was the loss of a developed consumer palate for fine wines. The wines produced during Prohibition were almost uniformly of poor quality and tended to be quite sweet. After repeal, the system for taxing alcoholic beverages favored wines, and as a consequence many producers concentrated on sweet, fortified wines that delivered the highest percentage of alcohol per retail dollar. For perhaps the first time in American history, wine became associated with the lower economic classes. "Winos" could get intoxicated from sweet dessert wines cheaper than from any other beverage. It was, in fact, not until 1961 that Americans again drank more table than dessert wine.

Finally, Prohibition lingers in Americans' historical consciousness as a symbol of many Protestant groups' continuing condemnation of alcohol consumption. Indeed, most Baptist, Methodist, and Disciple of Christ churches view the consumption of alcohol as a lapse in spiritual piety. This is even more stridently the case in such religious groups as the Latter-day Saints, Assemblies of God, Jehovah's Witnesses, and sundry Pentecostal denominations that currently rank among the fastest-growing religious bodies in the United States. When denouncing the consumption of alcoholic beverages, these groups generally focus upon health concerns more than on the preservation of stern piety, but their unflagging commitment to temperance continues to cast an aura of suspicion upon all those who find delight in a glass or two of wine. The pervasive influence of conservative Protestantism's moral outlook thus lingers in American culture. Brother Timothy of the late Christian Brothers Winery is a good example of a religiously oriented person's frustration with the all-or-nothing zeal that pervades the religious right's insistence upon prohibition. Brother Timothy worked tirelessly to educate the American public about the sanative effect of wine taken in moderation, and he never missed an opportunity to draw attention to the long association of wine and spirituality in the western cultural heritage. The T-shirt he had made displaying the phrase "Christ made wine . . . miraculously from water. He attached no warning label to that wine" expresses well his consternation at the neoprohibitionist attitudes that continue to plague the American wine industry. The famed California vintner Robert Mondavi likewise has tried to counter the prohibitionist sentiments emanating from conservative Protestant groups. In the early 1990s he prominently displayed a label on his wines that reminded consumers that "Wine has been with us since the beginning of civilization. It is the temperate, civilized, sacred, romantic, mealtime beverage recommended in the Bible. Wine has been praised for centuries by statesmen, philosophers, poets, and scholars. Wine in moderation is an integral part of our culture, heritage and the gracious way of life." The federal government's Bureau of Alcohol, Tobacco, and Firearms later insisted that the Mondavi winery cease attaching this label to its wines, claiming that these statements about the cultural heritage of wine are "unconfirmable."

In some respects, then, Prohibition's indiscriminate moral outlook has never totally disappeared from popular American culture. Rather than sharpening our vision of the personal and social evils of alcohol abuse, the virulent call to total Prohibition instead fostered ideological commitments that went well beyond any prudent concern for our individual or societal well-being. And, in attacking the enjoyment of wine, Prohibition declared a substance to be evil that had been associated with spirituality throughout most of the course of Western cultural history. But, as is so often the case, long-standing cultural traditions rarely disappear altogether. Instead, they reappear in new and innovative forms. Not only do many of our religious denominations continue to embrace the sacramental symbolism associated with wine, but also the enjoyment of wine in recent decades has given rise to a novel version of American "popular religion."

CHAPTER 5

Popular Religion and the Wine Revolution

The late 1960s witnessed the beginnings of a wine revolution in the United States. Annual wine consumption grew from a low of about 0.3 gallons per capita at the end of World War II to about 2.2 gallons in the early 1980s. Throughout the 1950s and 1960s Americans ordered cocktails while having dinner at a restaurant; yet, in the 1970s and 1980s, they learned to feel comfortable ordering wine while dining out. At home, too, a glass of wine in the evening has become a popular replacement for beer or highballs. Accompanying this rapid increase in per capita consumption of wine has been a decided shift to more sophisticated wines. As Americans became better educated about wine, there was a new and sustained consumer demand for wines made from premier varietal grapes. Indeed, it was only in 1968 that what might be called "dinner wines" first outsold the sweet or even syrupy wines that had emerged with Prohibition.

Between 1973 and 1984, over four hundred and fifty wineries opened up in North America to meet the burgeoning demand for quality varietal wines. These wineries, unlike their counterparts in the middle of the nineteenth century, were not built by immigrants trying to find their niche in the land of opportunity. Those who have pushed the revival of the American wine industry have come from the professional classes. Physicians, dentists, stockbrokers, attorneys, university professors, engineers, and media celebrities populate the list of those who have turned their avocation into a full- or part-time vocation. Many have entered the business as a hobby or as an exciting means of diversifying their investments. Others have found establishing a "boutique winery" to be a more rewarding alternative to their former careers. So successful has the industry been on the whole that now American vineyards are the envy of the world's most affluent entrepreneurs. Indeed, foreign corporations now own a substantial portion of the most prized vineyards in the United States.

It should not be surprising that the new generation of wine consumers in the United States is concentrated among professionals. Households headed by professionals consume an estimated half again as much wine as other households; white-collar households consume about 4.8 gallons annually compared to 1.6 gallons in blue-collar homes.[1] Many of these new wine enthusiasts were first introduced to wine during their college years in the 1960s and 1970s. Wine, far more than beer or hard liquor, was the form of alcohol most closely associated with the collegiate "counterculture." Pop wines, such as Ripple or Boone's Farm fruit wines, were commonplace on college campuses and at rock concerts. As these individuals grew older and their tastes and incomes matured, they gravitated toward drier, more sophisticated wine. The baby boomers, especially those in the white-collar ranks, were on the whole better educated than their parents. What is often called the Yuppie syndrome refers at least in part to the recent tendency of America's younger professional class to spend their income on items that they associated with prestige and quality, but also items they considered to be, in some way, more "natural." Wine, being less filling than beer and less incapacitating than hard liquor, fit well with the emerging tastes of a generation of Americans eager to adopt lifestyles that exuded both success and acquired taste.

American Wine Culture

The consumption and appreciation of wine among Americans has gradually given rise to a distinctively American "wine culture." By culture is meant the words, ritualized behaviors, and ceremonies that express—and shape—a people's understanding of themselves and the world they live in. A "culture" emerges from a people's ideas about character, their aesthetic style and mood, and the ideas they have about what makes something truly meaningful or significant. The words, behaviors, and ceremonies that express these ideas about life also have the ability to perpetuate them. That is, a culture provides individuals with patterned ways of thinking and acting, and, in this way, a culture structures a group's experience of the world. This is clearly the case with the culture that has grown up around wine drinking. Wine enthusiasts employ their own language, advocate their own behavioral codes, and engage in ceremonies or festivals that celebrate the finer things in life. A "wine culture" has been long grown in Western European nations among both the aristocracy, who consume finer wines, and the working class, who enjoy ordinary table wine and annual wine festivals. The wine culture that has emerged in American culture reveals much about the ways in which we have "creatively borrowed" from Western Europe and slowly developed a distinct social and aesthetic style.

One example of the emergence of a wine culture in the United States is the fact that, from the Atlantic to the Pacific Coasts, wine festivals have sprung up celebrating American wines.[2] Agricultural festivals are an ancient tradition. Most modern religious holidays began as ancient festivals commemorating various stages of the agricultural cycle. What is interesting about American wine festivals is that they appear in locations (e.g., New York City; Sea Island, Georgia; Aspen, Colorado; and Longboat Key, Florida) and on dates that have nothing to do with wine production. And, too, most are upscale affairs targeted to the wealthy. Attendance can cost a thousand dollars and more. These are not simple *Winzerfests* at which local farmers drink and dance at harvest time, such as can be found in villages all through Germany. In contrast, most American wine festivals consist of hours of lectures, seminars, and structured "blind tastings" whereby participants build skills at identifying wines by sight, coloration, and taste. These festivals symbolize America's growing enthusiasm for the celebration of fine food and wines. In this sense American wine culture parallels the aesthetic spirituality of Japanese religious life, with its reverent tea ceremonies in which the simple sharing of food and drink deepens participants' sense of the sacredness of personal relationships and of the divine character of nature's gifts. Yet, American wine festivals are also frequently gaudy affairs. Attendance at the premier "wine extravaganzas" held at posh New York or Los Angeles hotels can run into hundreds, even thousands, of dollars. These events feature not so much the pristine beauty of the wines but rather the dazzling affectations of the tasters themselves. The lavish banquets and endless parade of expensive wines numb the palate and make these events less a celebration of the wines than yet another commercially induced instance of conspicuous consumption.

In addition to the emergence of wine festivals, small tasting groups have sprouted up in nearly every city in the country.[3] What was for decades confined to a small number of connoisseurs has in recent years mushroomed into a loosely organized cult. Groups from two to a hundred persons gather regularly to sample wine from particular vintages, geographical regions, etc. Often held in connection with a gourmet food club meeting, wine tastings bring people together to share their personal reactions to "exquisite" sensory experiences. Wine enthusiasts summon their acquired storehouses of factual and experiential knowledge to help stimulate one another to ever new levels of heightened sensory appreciation. John Bender's description of a "blind tasting" captures the unique way in which wine-tasting groups resemble religious celebrations. A wine tasting, like a religious service designed to give rise to a felt sense of the holy, leads individuals through a series of ritualized behaviors that are designed to bring individuals face to face with that which is deemed perfect or exquisite:

> The sight of a dozen or more wine enthusiasts . . . bearing down on a table forested with glasses and studded with bottles in brown bags can strike any uninitiated participant with terror. More daunting still is the hushed concentration the celebrants may sustain for up to an hour while they study the wines, taking notes by systematic methods of observation and evaluation. Then comes the exacting discussion of virtue and vice in each liquid, during the course of which one may witness awesome displays of technical, geographical, and terminological knowledge. Finally, the dread moment of the ratings, when every wine but one is sacrificed on the altar of supremacy.[4]

The results of such wine tastings are in turn shared with friends, colleagues, and unsuspecting browsers at the local liquor store. Some wine enthusiasts rise to the rank of professional taster and earn a living writing newsletters that compile tasting notes, books that rate vintages and give advice to the beginner, or articles for national wine periodicals.[5] An arcane vocabulary that distinguishes initiates of the wine-tasting phenomenon is transmitted from master enologist to novice in these formal and informal ways. The essence of such "wine communication" is to communicate the romance and aesthetic delight of the sensory experience occasioned by the drinking of wine. In his *The Romance of Wine,* H. Warner Allen fairly effuses over the sensory delights of wine drinking: "Wine indeed appeals to all the senses except the sense of hearing. Apart from its elusive bouquet and complex aroma, a great wine presents to the eye the joy of colour and through the sense of touch flatters the palate and throat, not only with a refreshing sense of coolness and a grateful feeling of satisfaction due to its temperature and the fineness of its alcohol, but also with the incomparable softness of its velvety texture."[6]

There is an intricate relationship between a culture and the language in which it is encoded and communicated. "Wine talk" has its own semantic structure. Although conversation about wine often seems confusing to beginning wine drinkers, it has been systematically examined and found to contain a highly complex means of permitting communication about a very particular universe of human experience.[7] Various terms and phrases have emerged to denote the prototypical sensory experiences that are basic to our induction into wine culture. Consider, for example, how particular and culture-specific phrases can be used to accentuate the visual appearance of a wine (e.g., straw colored, cloudy, casting amber, long legs); its olfactory properties (e.g., fig and dough aromas, cherry and courant bouquet, rich on the nose); its oral sensations (e.g., very restrained but broad and soft on the palate, lean and citric but with depth to the flavors and a subtle texture that carries the flavors through to an impressively long finish, smooth and harmonious with a crisp acidity and long on the finish); and the wine's overall sensory quality (e.g., unusual and seductive, a powerhouse red, pedestrian for a Napa chardonnay, lean and firm, youthful and earthy but not rough). Wine tasters are in this sense much like the religious mystic. Like the mystic, wine tasters are committed to the essentially ineffable nature of a private experience of something that is both ephemeral and ethereal. Yet, also like the mystic, they nonetheless exist in communities or traditions in which certain words or phrases come to signify, and possibly even elicit, prototypical sensations.

There are numerous other expressions of contemporary American wine culture. For example, wine enthusiasts make pilgrimages to favorite viticultural regions. In California, Napa Valley ranks second only to Disneyland in terms of the number of annual tourists. Visitors tour the vineyards, examine the production facilities, and then sample wines—many of which can be procured only at the winery. Surrounding the central act of pilgrimage in typically American fashion are souvenir shops, expensive restaurants, health spas, and balloon or tram rides. Relics in the form of rare wines and colorful T-shirts serve as emblems of the pilgrim's adventure.

Another manifestation of American wine culture has been the renewal of belief in the medicinal properties of wine. Much about a culture can be learned from its medical beliefs. Medical beliefs reveal underlying assumptions about what a culture believes to be the "real" forces or causes upon which human well-being depends. The idea that wine has therapeutic value is a long-standing belief in Western culture. Throughout the history of Judaism, wine has been placed at "the head of all medicine." The rabbinical tradition has been wary of overreliance upon drugs and instructs instead that "[o]nly where there is no wine are drugs required."[8] In the New Testament Paul counsels Timothy to "take a little wine for thy stomach's sake and for thy frequent infirmities." The Roman Catholic Church has owned vineyards in nearly every major viticultural region and used wines to treat the local citizenry. Even the Volstead Act accommodated the continuing use of wine-based tonics and permitted the sale of wine for medicinal value. Yet, mainstream twentieth-century American medicine has given little credence to the medicinal value of wine and has tended to dismiss such claims as owing to "subjective" or "psychological" and, by implication, imaginary causes. The "holistic health" movement in the 1960s and 1970s drew Americans' attention away from a purely materialistic medical outlook and once again highlighted the causal influences of attitudes, mental states, and beliefs upon physical health. It is not coincidental that part and parcel of this movement was a resurfacing of interest in wine as a therapeutic agent. Books such as *A History of Wine as Therapy* (1963), *Wine Is the Best Medicine* (1974), and *Stay Healthy with Wine* (1981) are examples of the growing tendency among American wine drinkers to acknowledge openly their belief that wine—like divine spirit—is a force that promotes life and that can inwardly empower wine drinkers to express life in a more abundant way.[9] These works, incidentally, tend to promote holistic approaches to human health. They tout the physiological properties of wine (e.g., the various vitamins and minerals they contain), the mental benefits of wine drinking (e.g., relaxation, calmness, optimistic outlook), and the overall lifestyle that comes from the enjoyment of wine (e.g., vibrant good health, an appreciation of life's hidden pleasures, and even heightened sexual virility and enjoyment of "wildly beautiful climaxes").

In recent years public interest in this connection between wine and health has grown considerably. In 1991 the popular press began publicizing scientific data chronicling the relatively low incidence of heart disease among the French, despite the fact that their diets are traditionally high in fat, they characteristically shun rigorous exercise, and a high percentage of them smoke cigarettes. This phenomenon, known as the "the French paradox," drew new attention to the positive effects of drinking alcohol, particularly red wine, as part of a daily diet. American physicians David Whitten and Martin Lipp maintain that the scientific evidence from the "French paradox" and other studies strongly suggests that "light, regular wine consumption" lowers the overall risk of death due to cardiovascular disease. Their exploration of the health benefits of wine, entitled *To Your Health*, makes a strong argument that, in moderation, daily wine drinking has a positive effect on our digestive systems, cardiovascular systems, overall nutrition, and emotional well-being.[10] Carefully argued endorsements of wine's medical benefits, such as Whitten and Lipp's, not only reinforce American's recent interest in holistic approaches to health but also revive Western culture's century-old heritage of viewing wine as the vital link between humanity's physical, emotional, and spiritual natures.

Wine is also closely connected to artistic expression.[11] Wine and wine drinking have been the subjects of a variety of works in the visual arts for nearly three thousand years of Western cultural history. The ancient Greeks and Romans depicted their gods enjoying wine. Jesus often chose the metaphor of "toiling in the vineyard" as a rhetorical device for depicting pure, wholesome activity. Christian artists have for centuries chosen to represent this theme of Christian teachings visually by incorporating pictorial scenes of vineyards into their paintings. Even in paintings that have no overt religious meaning, grapes and wine are frequently incorporated as symbols of serenity and purity. For example, "still life" paintings often focus on bunches of grapes or on some variation of the "jug of wine, a loaf of bread, and thou" theme. Similarly, landscape paintings with rolling vineyards, mythological characters engaged in a bacchanalian feast, or human laborers in a vineyard gracing their lives by work—all express the artistic representations of wine culture throughout Western history.

Only in comparatively recent years have American artists discovered and given distinctively American expression to these themes. American artistic talent is revealed on the thousands of wine labels that are designed to affix to the bottles of each year's new vintage. Although it might be premature to pronounce wine labels as the key to a distinctive American aesthetics, they nonetheless contain a fusion of elements that is highly suggestive: the overt ties with American religious history via missionlike wineries, an attraction to bold graphics, a sensibility for American scenery or locales, an overt tongue-in-cheek humor, and a continuous effort to imitate French standards of high culture despite endless protestations of having found our own unique wine-making style.[12] Artistic wine labels are themselves certainly not original with American vintners. Baron Philippe de Rothschild, proprietor of Chateau Mouton Rothschild in France's Bordeaux district, has for many years commissioned noted artists to design labels for his esteemed cabernets. In 1977 Marty Lee, one of the owners of the prestigious Kenwood Vineyards in Sonoma County, commissioned a San Francisco artist to help commemorate the release of Kenwood's special cabernet. The artist, David Lance Goines, was given a free hand and designed a "Naked Lady" for the label. When the label was submitted to the Bureau of Alcohol, Tobacco, and Firearms for approval, Kenwood received the following reply: "The drawing of the young lady must be deleted. More specifically the Bureau regards the picture as 'obscene and indecent' under regulations 27cKR 4.39 (a) (3). . . ."

This was, ironically, the rather inauspicious beginning to what was to become a renowned collection of American art. The Kenwood Vineyard "Artist Series" has graced the American wine industry with a significant display of American visual art. Featuring a different American artist each year, this series reveals a broad range of aesthetic style from still life, serene landscapes, and alluring abstract imagery. This overt intention of celebrating the natural affinity of great wine and the fine arts also draws attention to the very real sense in which wine making is itself an art form. The selection of grapes, the harvesting process, direction of the fermentation process, and intuitive judgments concerning the blending and aging of wine all reveal the controlled creativity whereby a wine maker turns grapes into a product meant for aesthetic enjoyment. Of course, all wine is not artistic any more than all painting is. But the same repertoire of artistic skill is needed: technical mastery of tools, wisdom garnered through experience, a playful willingness to take risks and resist becoming constrained by the tools or equipment with which one creates.

Wine Culture as Popular Religion

In all of this it is possible to detect a religious quality to Americans' celebration of life. Through tasting groups, festivals, gourmet dinners, therapeutic beliefs, and label art, wine has become a vehicle for what scholars of religion refer to as "cultural" or "popular" religion.[13] Cultural religion differs from churched religion in that it has no distinct institutional or theological boundaries. It consists not of formal theology, but of a people's spontaneous tendency to create new means of celebrating life, of treasuring things for their intrinsic significance rather than their instrumental value, and of pushing beyond the boundaries of daily routine to catch glimpses of the innate beauty of human existence. None of this necessarily entails beliefs about the afterlife. Nor does it require recognition of a god or revealed scripture. But whenever a culture provides a means whereby people might voice their quest for both ecstasy and community, it is important to recognize the religious dimension of that spontaneous cultural creation.

The fact that American wine culture expresses many overtly religious qualities is not difficult to explain or understand. After all, it has grown naturally out of a long-lasting religiocultural heritage in Western history. The cult of Dionysos or Bacchus, the god of wine, was very much a part of the world-embracing heritage that ancient Greece and Rome bequeathed to Western Civilization. The roots of institutionalized religion have been no less saturated with wine. Most Jewish holidays began originally as spontaneous cultural celebrations of the agricultural cycle and were always accompanied by wine consumption. In early Judaism wine was poured out as a libation during the sacrificial rituals offered to Yahweh, and, to this day, wine remains a central part of the celebration of the Seder meal during Passover. Jewish scriptures positively embrace the consumption of wine as a good that is only spoiled if taken to the point of drunkenness. The Old Testament proclaims that an abundance of wine is a blessing from God.[14] An extraordinary abundance is thought to be nothing less than a sign of the Messianic Age.[15] Indeed, the Old Testament is forthright in its endorsement of the mood elevation and "gladdening of the heart" that wine offers.[16]

The turning of water into wine was said to be Jesus's first public miracle. Roman Catholics believe that, at his last Passover meal, Christ changed bread and wine into his body and blood. And, in fact, the very power of apostolic succession upon which the Roman Catholic Church operates is based upon the belief that Christ conferred this same power of transforming bread and wine to his successors. Throughout most of Christian history, the central act of worship has been Holy Communion, which focuses upon the holy significance of wine as a vehicle to God's gracious spirit. Even in the nonsacramental or "low" Protestant traditions, wine (or at the very least unfermented grape juice) is still symbolic of the gathering of humans into a united community. As Rabbi Leo Trapp has put it, "Catholic as well as Jewish tradition makes it impossible to establish a community of religious people where wine cannot be obtained. Wine is part of worship, symbol and expression of the human and the divine."[17]

The contemporary wine revolution has built upon this historical heritage and given it new celebratory expressions. True, these new expressions are neither openly nor doctrinally religious. But they are nonetheless concrete instances of Americans' quest for ecstasy, community, and for a fuller participation in life's intrinsic pleasures. A religion—whether institutional or popular—can generally be thought of as having creeds, a moral code, and a distinctive form of worship or cultus. Wine culture, as an expression of popular religion, does in fact exhibit such a creed, code, and cultus. The creeds of wine culture are numerous. They pertain first and foremost to beliefs about what makes any given wine truly excellent. Learning these creeds requires years of catechism-like study and instruction. Sectarian opinions exist, of course, but there is nonetheless a kind of inherited orthodoxy about the respective roles of climate, aging, relative proportion of residual sugar to acidity, etc. There are also creeds that pertain to an individual's progressive development as one who is "worthy" of appreciating the subtle nuances that distinguish a good wine from a truly great wine. Acquired mastery of such cultural lore is even thought to be a prerequisite to entrance into the higher orders of wine-tasting delight. As H. Warner Allen describes it,

"Our joy of the world is increased by an understanding of the artistic pleasure that a great wine can give, and a great wine cannot be fully appreciated without some knowledge of its composition."[18]

Associated with these creeds is the code that governs etiquette or propriety among wine drinkers. The code specifies behavioral norms that are to be disregarded only at grave cost to one's "enological purity." Among other things, this code stipulates proper techniques for storing wine, removing the cork, decanting and pouring wine, the selection of appropriate glasses, and the pairing of wines with appropriate foods. It also stipulates behaviors (e.g., smoking or excessive alcohol consumption) that are to be avoided because they will impair the palate and corrupt the wine-tasting experience as such.

The heart of wine culture, and what most closely distinguishes its religious dimensions, is the ritual, or cultus, of tasting. Wine tasting provides an almost paradigmatic example of what anthropologist Victor Turner has described as the transformative power of rituals. By this phrase, Turner means that nearly every society gives rise to its own unique rituals that mediate between two somewhat opposing ways in which humans relate to each other.[19] The first of these he calls "structure." The "structural" dimension of human existence refers to the laws, rules, and formal institutions that regulate social existence. Because humans will always compete for limited economic resources, there is a need for social structures capable of regulating our relationships in ways that minimize conflict. The structures of society impose certain roles, responsibilities, ethical duties, and behavioral codes upon us for the purpose of communal stability. Yet, these very structures accentuate the differences between us and have an inherent tendency to drain us of our vitality and of any uncoerced spirit of friendship and love. Further, because social structures channel our relationships with others into role-bound patterns of interaction, they foster a certain impersonality in communal life. In this sense, "structure" tends to deplete us of our most human qualities and over time leads to resentments, friction, and dispiritedness.

Turner refers to the second major mode of human existence as "communitas." Communitas consists of those spontaneous bonds of friendship and love without which there could be no society. It is the spirit of our fundamental unity with others that fosters care and concern for our fellow human beings. According to Turner, communitas is felt as a distinct mode of consciousness, set apart from our workaday life amidst social structures. Communitas breaks into human lives in those moments when we have temporarily suspended our structured habits of thought and action. There is a distinctively religious quality to the experience of communitas, and, in fact, Turner notes that almost everywhere humans attribute communitas to the influx of a divine spirit into the human realm. Communitas reinvigorates lives that have been drained of vitality by the rigidities of social structure. It transforms the "I-It" character of role-structured relationships into "I-Thou" encounters characterized by selfless love. And, finally, communitas infects individual life with a sense of boundless, mystical power capable of stimulating us to new levels of growth and creativity.

According to Turner, it is the function of a ritual to release individuals temporarily from life in structure and provide them with a felt sense of communitas. Rituals thus function within a culture by providing a framework for reinvigorating individual life and renewing our sensibility for the precious quality of interpersonal relationships. The sharing of wine is, as we shall see, uniquely suited to serve these ritual functions. It brings individuals together outside their accustomed social and economic roles to savor something of exquisite beauty that has no real utilitarian purpose other than the grace it sheds upon our appreciation of life. It was in connection with this ritual quality of wine that a journalist and man of letters, George Saintsbury, recollected that when the wines he had consumed "were good they pleased my senses, cheered my spirits, improved my moral and intellectual powers, besides enabling me to confer the same benefits on other people."[20]

Wine tasting's ritualistic features also foster its aesthetic dimension. Wine engages the senses and invites individuals to perceive and appreciate natural pleasures. More importantly, wine tasting elicits from individuals the felt conviction that the "excellence" they strive to behold resides simultaneously in the aesthetic object (the wine) and in themselves, the subject of the aesthetic experience. This fusion of subject and object is the prototypical characteristic of all mystical experiences and is undoubtedly induced in part by the slight alteration in consciousness promoted by the alcohol content of wine. It is also nurtured by the ritualized activity surrounding the tasting experience. The opening of the bottle, the long period of expectancy while the wine is allowed to "breathe," and each successive step of judging the wine's color, bouquet, and impressions on the palate all create a unique setting in which the individual ritually merges with the object of his or her devotion. And, too, this ritual serves to "fund" the immediate sensory experience with memories and acquired knowledge. Each sensation engages memories of previous tastings, which, in turn, contribute to the fund of sensory impressions. For a brief moment the wine taster struggles to abstract specific elements from the immediate sensory experience and to consider how they might correlate with an acquired repertoire of knowledge concerning the possible ways in which climate, soil, production technology, specific varietal characteristics, bottle aging, or temperature influence a wine's sensory qualities. These memories and abstract considerations in turn focus our attention in ways that restructure, heighten, and invest our sensory experience with meaning. In and through this aesthetic experience, the individual is alternating rapidly between a mode of receptivity to incoming stimuli and an active attempt to sort out and interpret this stimuli. The experience is, for this reason, exhilarating. It unites our intellectual and experiential faculties in ways that impart a sense of synergy and vibrancy.

The lure of this wine-tasting ritual is not hard to understand. The aesthetic dimension of human experience—the sense of opening up to and directly participating in a higher order of beauty or excellence—is perhaps the least developed element in the American psyche. Our competitive capitalism and our highly ascetic (i.e., moralistic) religious ethos do little to help individuals learn to let down the rigid boundaries of ego and to merge experientially with some nonphysical, or "higher," reality. Even in America's more ritualistic religious groups, such as Roman Catholicism, Episcopalianism, and Orthodox Judaism, the availability of aesthetic experience is problematic to many because of its overt connections with an intellectual heritage that can seem too confining. Importantly, wine drinking provides thousands of Americans with an aesthetic experience that provides them with momentary freedom from their normal cognitive and practical functions. In the contemplation of an elegant wine they become free to play with their imaginations and to exercise their capacities to delight in beauty for its own sake. In his analysis of the formal philosophical properties of aesthetics, Charles Senn Taylor writes, "A wine which truly animates the representative powers does so through the complex smells, tastes, and colors which it provides for contemplation. The more complex those factors are, the more we are likely to linger over them, to meditate upon them—and the more the wine will be able to keep up with, to sustain, to even strengthen our meditation."[21]

Aesthetics and spirituality are intimately interwoven. A developed aesthetic sensibility might even be argued to be a kind of experiential prerequisite to a fully developed spirituality. That is, a felt sense of a higher order of things underlies and provides the zest for a spiritual attitude toward life. It should thus not at all surprise us that wine drinking somewhat inadvertently begins to open up a very genuine, if unchurched, spirituality in many middle- and upper-class Americans. The "cultus" of wine drinking appeals to a certain yearning for personal initiation into Nature's "higher reaches." The appeal of wine drinking might well be considered a contemporary instance of what American historian Catherine Albanese terms the "nature religion" that has provided a compelling religious center to American culture throughout our history.[22] That is, for over two hundred years, Americans, including such luminaries as Thomas Jefferson, Ralph Waldo Emerson, Henry David Thoreau, and John Muir, have sensed the moral and spiritual dimensions of a direct encounter with Nature. Many of our alternative healing systems, natural diets, and ecological convictions in some way participate in this perduring conviction that human fulfillment ultimately depends upon our ability to live in harmony with the hidden spiritual dimensions of Nature. Wine drinking is a type of ritual that makes it possible for individuals to suspend their secular identities and to create an awareness of levels of natural beauty that exist at a level too subtle to be appreciated by the calculating ego of our normal waking consciousness. In his masterpiece on humanity's propensity for religion, *The Varieties of Religious Experience*, William James noted that alcohol produces a distinct altered state of consciousness that should be considered "one bit of the mystic consciousness, and our total opinion of it must find its place in our opinion of that larger whole."[23] James believed:

> [T]he sway of alcohol over mankind is unquestionably due to its power to stimulate the mystical faculties of human nature, usually crushed to earth by the cold facts and dry criticism of the sober hour. Sobriety diminishes, discriminates, and says no; drunkenness expands, unites, and says yes. It is in fact the great exciter of the *Yes* function in man. It brings its votary from the chill periphery of things to the radiant core. It makes him for the moment one with the truth.[24]

As James suggested, alcohol helps dismantle what might be called our "general reality orientation," with its built-in mechanisms for separating reality into discrete bits or into objects of experience that can be manipulated for the purpose of better adapting to or exploiting our environment. Wine does this in a much less pronounced way than hard liquor. The self, therefore, is not so much dissolved as reconfigured in ways that make possible a more aesthetic sense of relatedness. Instrumental reason is temporarily in abeyance, and awareness is instead flooded with a sense of relatedness to life's intrinsic meanings and pleasures. As James describes this in another of his studies of religious awareness, in the altered state of consciousness produced by mild alcohol intoxication, "the centre and periphery of things seem to come together. The ego and its objects, the *meum* and the *teum*, are one."[25] This aesthetic sense of union and communion is the experiential basis of the religious longing for initiation into Nature's higher reaches. Wine culture, as with other forms of American popular or cultural religion, simply carries this yearning for a deeper harmony with Nature into a less overtly "religious" setting than do the sacraments of our established churches. Yet, this form of American popular religion, no less than this country's "churched" religion, embodies and combines our desire for immediate contact with Nature and for the creation of community.

In sum, the flourishing of wine culture during the last few decades bears the distinctive traits of a genuinely spiritual movement within American culture. It does not, of course, compete with, or in any way replace, "theological" religion with its important articulation of doctrinal and moral guides to life. Nor is this spirituality in any way to be commended unreservedly, given the fact that it is largely captive to commercial forces and is closely associated with unabashed consumerism and self-indulgence. But the wine revolution has given bold new expression to the long-neglected aesthetic side of American cultural life. The gradual mingling of religious and secular forces shaping Americans' attitudes toward wine drinking has given rise to a wine culture that has enabled many modern Americans to appreciate the exhilaration that comes from an enhanced openness to natural sensations and from sharing these inner experiences in a communal context.

Religion and Wine

CONCLUDING OBSERVATIONS

The close connection between religion and wine throughout the course of American history calls for some final attempt, however humble, at constructing helpful generalizations and concluding interpretations. The fact that a beverage can be invested with symbolic meaning is itself a fairly widespread anthropological phenomenon. This is, of course, particularly true of intoxicating beverages insofar as they open up wholly new areas of experience that impart sensations of ecstasy, enthusiasm, and vision. Yet, as Bruce Lincoln has explained, even quite ordinary beverages have come to be celebrated in myth, ritual, and sacred speculation.[1] Milk, for example, is almost universally associated with both the sustenance of life and family nurturance and thus frequently becomes invested with religious significance. In many passages of Hebrew scripture, milk is depicted as a paradisiacal fluid, and Israel is even referred to as "the land of milk and honey." Lincoln also observes:

> [A]mong the Maasai and other cattle-herding peoples of East Africa, cow's milk is a staple part of the diet, but it is nevertheless regarded with the greatest of respect, for unlike virtually all other food items, milk can be obtained without causing the death of any living thing, animal or vegetable. For this reason, milk is set in marked contrast to beef, a food which has the same source as milk—cattle—but the procurement of which entails the violent death of the animal from which it is taken. The equation is explicitly drawn: milk is to meat as life is to death, and the two are not to be mixed within the same meal.[2]

Similar kinds of connections undoubtedly account for the close connection of wine with spirituality in the Western cultural heritage. Since 4000 B.C.E., wine has been associated with family meals. It is only natural, then, that wine gradually became linked with domestic solidarity, interpersonal warmth, and shared values. We might also note how wine, like many other agricultural products, symbolizes the union of divine and human activities. That is, the growing of grapes and the production of wine require a harmonious blending of human and divine activities. The grapevine itself has, since biblical times, been viewed as a gift from God and as a symbol of the divine benevolence we find throughout Nature. Thus the grapes themselves, as well as the presence of wild yeasts that initiate the fermentation process, are a part of nature's creative rhythms. Humans can, however, join with God's creative activity by nurturing these natural processes. Vines can be pruned and cultivated, fermentation can be carefully monitored, and in this way human ingenuity can help produce wines of a higher quality than unassisted nature would have produced. In this sense the production of wine, unlike that of distilled spirits, is representative of humanity's close connection with nature's spontaneous capacity to sustain and enhance human life. Wine is, furthermore, a beverage that goes through a "life cycle" that closely parallels that of humans: fresh and untamed in youth, mellowing to maturity in mid-cycle, and continuing to show broad signs of its best qualities even as it ages into final dissolution. It is thus easy to see why wine has historically been associated with the celebration of life and used in ceremonies commemorating significant rites of passage.

Wine would also appear to have certain distinctive characteristics that give it an almost singular ability to foster celebratory social interaction and communal bonding. We might return to anthropologist Victor Turner's distinction between "life in structure" and "life in communitas." By "structure" Turner means to draw attention to the fact that in one important sense humans are in competition with one another for life's limited resources. As a consequence, a good deal of social interaction is defined by the legal and economic structures that define the ways through which we might pursue our individual purposes. Yet, as Turner observes, there is more to human existence than the competitive pursuit of our utilitarian needs. The term communitas is his shorthand expression for modes of noncompetitive human interaction that are experienced as intrinsically meaningful. Turner contends that when ritually released from normal social roles and structures, humans spontaneously experience a certain rejuvenation and spontaneity, accompanied by a sense of interpersonal relatedness that Turner describes as the "essential and genuine human bond, without which there could be no society."[3] The sharing of wine provides precisely the kind of ritual activity that fosters a shift from structured, utilitarian human interaction to the kind of nonutilitarian, extended sociality that makes up communitas. First, the subtle flavors and textures of wine are so nuanced as to engage individuals in discussions concerning a given wine's aesthetic merits. Wine is for this reason uniquely suited to transforming a meal into an extended mode of sociality. Consider, for example, how frequently wine was present at meal times in the hardworking communal societies such as New Harmony, the Amana colonies, and the early settlements of the Latter-day Saints. In the case of the Amana colonies, not only was wine drinking present at major religious services and at communal meals, but it was also the focus of small gatherings of men who spent their Sabbath day of rest discussing the merits of their homemade wines.

This linkage of wine with religious worship, communal meals, and informal gatherings would appear to be perfect confirmation of anthropologist Mary Douglas's observation that "the meaning of a meal is found in a system of repeated analogies." That is, there is a mutually reinforcing relationship between the ways in which wine is associated with community, aesthetic delight, and religious worship. The symbolic associations of wine in one setting (e.g., in communal dining or ritualized worship) have a direct effect upon wine's meaning in another. In this way the meaning of consuming wine in any one context is embedded in a much wider system of "analogies" that accentuate its symbolic role in mediating between the mundane and the extraordinary, the secular and the sacred. In her essay "Deciphering a Meal," Douglas argues that distinctive forms of eating contain their own implicit cultural meanings and that "each meal is a structured social event which structures others in its own image."[4] A community's ritual use of wine thus seems to be an effective means of fostering wider patterns of social interaction characterized by the felt presence of interpersonal warmth, or communitas. From established denominations, such as Roman Catholicism or Judaism, to newly emerging religious communities, such as Thomas Lake Harris's Brotherhood Colony or the early Latter-day Saints, the communal sharing of wine has helped structure other forms of social interaction in ways that foster a mingling of the individual and the community, the mundane and the extraordinary, the secular and the sacred.

Wine also contains what might possibly be an "ideal" level of alcohol for engaging individuals in spirited collegiality. Containing a slightly higher percentage of alcohol than beer, but far less than distilled spirits, wine has for centuries served to produce good cheer and celebratory emotions while avoiding the antisocial behaviors frequently associated with drunken excess (possibly owing to the typical pattern of consuming wine slowly over longer periods of time and with plentiful amounts of food, thereby reducing its inebriating potential). Whether it is the relative expense of wine, the cultural connection with sacramental attitudes, or its particular level of alcohol, the American historical record would seem to indicate that it is linked not only with the communal celebration of life, but with temperance as well.

A full understanding of the connection of religion and wine in the American context must also take into consideration the centuries-old association of wine with religious worship and sacramental expectations. We might begin pursuing the reasons for this association by remembering that even a relatively simple and nonalcoholic beverage such as tea has been invested with sacramental meanings in Japanese culture. Indeed, the very preparation, serving, and drinking of teas has been considered both an art form and a means of spiritual knowledge and liberation in Japan. As Bruce Lincoln observes in his assessment of the role of beverages in world religious history, Japanese tea masters have sought to create "nothing less than a perfect microcosm, a thoroughly harmonious environment in which one might take refuge from the tribulation of the external world and encounter the Buddha nature that lies beyond the conflicts and fluctuations of life in the material world."[5] We should not, of course, overlook the role that concentrated doses of caffeine might play in the production of this aesthetic spirituality. Yet, whatever the precise mix of contributing factors might be, Japanese tea ceremonies—like the sharing of bread and wine in the Western world—ritually reenact a harmonious blending of Heaven and Earth.

Wine, perhaps even more than tea, is a beverage intrinsically capable of affording individuals the sense that they are—however fragmentarily—partaking of divinity. The mild alteration of normal waking rationality induced by moderate wine consumption tends to give persons the conviction that they have momentarily transcended their normal mental and emotional powers; they feel themselves bestowed with a special gift of speech, enthusiasm, vitality, and well-being. As William James put it, mild alcohol consumption "expands, unites, and says yes. It is in fact the great exciter of the *Yes* function in man. . . . It makes him for the moment one with the truth."[6] Indeed, as Victor Turner has pointed out, the spontaneous experience of communitas such as often produced by wine drinking inevitably gives rise to the sense of communing with powers that are "more than human."[7]

And such has surely been the case in the American context. The historical record of wine consumption in the United States chronicles a recurring tendency to view wine in an Emersonian, Transcendentalism-like fashion. By this I mean that the aesthetic pleasures of wine drinking have prompted countless numbers of individuals to a conviction similar to Ralph Waldo Emerson's dictum that "Nature is the symbol of spirit." Emerson believed that it was possible for every human being to become deeply receptive to the spiritual powers underlying the creative rhythms of Nature. For him, Nature constitutes "the organ through which the universal spirit speaks to the individual, and strives to lead back the individual to it."[8] According to Emerson's Transcendentalist philosophy, then, any element of nature might potentially move a person to the aesthetic perception of his or her direct participation in the "universal spirit." And, indeed, there is ample historical evidence for the existence of a distinct strand of American "nature religion" centered around the aesthetic enjoyment of wine. Beginning with the restrained romanticism surrounding Thomas Jefferson's and Benjamin Franklin's enjoyment of wine to the Summum community's belief in the ability of wine to communicate higher forms of spiritual consciousness, wine drinking has prompted Americans to open themselves up to what the Japanese might call a harmonious blending of Heaven and Earth. The nineteenth-century mystic Thomas Lake Harris's belief that his wines released the "finer electro-vinous spirit" and were "infused with the divine aura, potentialized in the joy spirit" is certainly another example of the way in which wine drinking has been connected with metaphysical beliefs concerning the intimate connection between the natural and spiritual orders of life. So, too, was the experience of the Lutheran minister Friedrich Muench, whose pioneering efforts on behalf of the Missouri wine industry were accompanied by his abiding interest in Emerson's Transcendentalist writings. Muench's incorporation of Emerson's nature religion into his own theological views is plainly seen in his conviction that wine drinking permits individuals to have "daily intercourse with peaceful nature." Muench's Missouri contemporary, George Husmann, was no less convinced of the sacramental perspective that wine affords when, in a lecture on viniculture, he encouraged his listeners "to look from nature to nature's God." And thus from the Amana colonies' association of wine with their identity as "inspirationalists" to contemporary social gatherings of "wine buffs," wine drinking has joined our dual religious desires for having immediate contact with Nature (and Nature's God) and for creating a close-knit community.

This proclivity of wine for eliciting sacramental attitudes also helps us better understand the patterns of wine use—or nonuse—by various American religious groups. In chapter 3 we observed that the further religious groups are from the theological mainstream, the more they have tended to take strident attitudes for or against the religious use of wine. Most of the religious groups belonging to the "Protestant-Catholic-Jew" religious establishment in the United States have preserved the Western religious heritage's association of wine with the worship of God. Most of these denominations (e.g., Roman Catholicism, the Episcopal

Church, Presbyterianism, United Church of Christ, Lutheranism, and Reform, Orthodox, and Conservative Judaism) approach wine with a certain sacramental reverence and ritually incorporate its aesthetic properties into their traditional forms of worship. This, of course, continues the mystique that surrounds wine drinking in American culture as a whole, even among the nonreligious. Yet, as we have observed, religious groups that vary either theologically or demographically from the mainstream establishment have tended to demarcate themselves at least in part by their distinctive attitudes toward the drinking of wine.

While there is no simple generalization that covers the various reasons why some "sectarian" religious groups have embraced wine drinking more than is found in the more historically dominant denominations, it is clear that wine has performed at least three distinct functions in the creation and preservation of American sectarian groups. First, wine has clearly served to commemorate and foster the communal affirmation that has been so central in the formation of many American religious communities. The use of wine in the Amana colonies, among the Rappites, and in the early years of the Latter-day Saints testifies to the ability of wine to forge a felt sense of social solidarity. Insofar as wine fosters forms of social interaction that enable a more open display of warmth and affection than is ordinarily displayed in day-to-day living, it both symbolizes and elicits the kind of communitas that give newly emerging religious groups their almost palpable sense of shared love and enthusiasm.

Secondly, the mental changes induced by wine drinking favor the kind of "variation in ideas" that is often necessary to embolden individuals to strike out in theological directions that veer from the established churches. The enjoyment of wine while being engaged in lively discussions of religion and philosophy was, as we have seen, common among colonial intellectuals, such as Franklin and Jefferson, who became known for their free-thinking approach to religious issues. Thomas Lake Harris, Friedrich Muench, and George Husmann also leap out from the pages of our historical chronicle as examples of individuals known for their love of wine and for their commitment to bold religious and moral-political views. So, too, in a way, were those who participated in the 1960s "hippie culture" and gathered to smoke marijuana and drink pop wines while experimenting with a variety of novel religious and philosophical ideas. Wine loosens the hold of our normal patterns of waking thought and thereby encourages the very kind of intellectual experimentation that is a prerequisite to making a conscious decision to embrace variant religious beliefs.

Third, and finally, wine also promotes the formation of novel religious groups by providing individuals with a sense of emotional expansiveness. Alcoholic beverages are intrinsically capable of giving individuals the sense that they have transcended their ordinary mental and emotional powers and have suddenly been granted superior intellect and enhanced spiritual well-being. This enthusiasm tends to lessen the inhibitions that might otherwise counter any tendency to go against prevailing community opinion and embrace a novel religious path. Small wonder, then, that the more variant a religious group's theology or communal ethics are the more likely they are—especially in their formative stages—to benefit from their members' communal drinking of wine.

The very properties of wine that have fostered its incorporation into the life of some American religious communities simultaneously help account for the reasons why other religious groups have considered it a taboo. We might first focus on the sociological or cultural dimension of some American religious groups' restrictions against the use of wine. For example, kosher proscriptions concerning avoiding wines made by non-Jews and Joseph Smith's admonition against drinking wine that was "not made new among you" reveal religious groups' concern with distancing their members from the kind of intimate social interactions that might arise from drinking wine with nonmembers. Even more interesting, however, is the sociological boundary setting found in conservative Protestant groups' prohibition of wine drinking. The rise of "ascetic Protestantism" in the nineteenth century among many Baptists, Methodists, and Disciples of Christ was part and parcel of an emerging religious resistance to many features or trends surfacing in wider American culture. These religious groups, and their twentieth-century "holiness" counterparts, such as the Church of God and the Church of the Nazarene, represent a prophetic call against the secularizing influences of modern society. The piety these groups seek to instill in their members encourages a certain withdrawal or distancing from the intellectual trends (e.g., Darwinism and secular humanism), social trends (e.g., immigration and the breakdown of traditional authority structures), and lifestyle trends (e.g., the wide-scale repudiation of traditional moral codes) of modern life. Because they are concerned with erecting boundaries that protect against assimilation to the wider patterns of American culture, evangelical groups are also concerned with protecting against the very intellectual and emotional exuberance associated with wine drinking. The taboo against wine drinking, then, functions to preserve a certain "over and againstness" through which these groups differentiate themselves from the potential corruptions of an apostate world.

There is, of course, also a theological dimension to these groups' opposition to the consumption of wine. Strict evangelical faith considers improperly directed emotions to be the root of much of humanity's sinful behavior. The theological conceptions of salvation found in most American religious groups that oppose the use of wine drinking are predominantly evangelical. That is, they adamantly insist that there is nothing that humans can do to merit salvation. Because salvation is thought to proceed only from God's saving grace, it follows that no ritual action or emotional "opening" on the part of humans can, in and of itself, bring humans closer to God. It is interesting to note in this context that both Mary Douglas and Mircea Eliade have observed that a community's conceptions of taboo and uncleanliness frequently entail efforts to prevent individuals from having direct access to the divine.[9] Evangelical faith is predicated upon a wide gulf separating humanity from God, bridgeable only by the saving grace of Christ. From this perspective, the "spontaneous communitas" directly produced by wine is not only a misdirection of humanity's desire for communion with the sacred, but an action that is intrinsically unclean or even diabolic. In short, wine drinking is considered incompatible with conservative gospel faith.

In all, then, the connection of religion and wine in the American context provides a fascinating handle upon the nation's cultural history. Over and beyond the role of religious groups in pioneering American viniculture, wine has itself performed vital functions in the shaping of American religious life—both within and without the boundaries of established denominations.

Notes

Introduction

1. There are several reliable reference books on American wine. Leon Adams, *The Wines of America* (New York: McGraw-Hill Book Co., 1973), contains the most cultural and historical information and was very helpful in the research for this book. Doris Muscatine, Maynard Amerine, and Bob Thompson, eds., *The University of California/Sotheby Book of California Wine* (Berkeley, Calif.: University of California Press, 1984), contains approximately fifty essays that collectively address nearly every aspect of California wines. Standard reference books that discuss the role of climate, soil, and technology in wine making and include chapters specifically devoted to American wine are Hugh Johnson, *The World Atlas of Wine* (New York: Simon and Schuster, 1977), and Andre Simon, ed., *Wines of the World* (New York: McGraw-Hill Publishing, 1972). Readers might also wish to consult Anthony Dias Blue, *American Wine: A Comprehensive Guide* (New York: Harper and Row, 1988), and Peter Quimme, *The Signet Book of American Wine* (New York: Signet Books, 1979).
2. Ronald Siegel presents a colorful overview of humanity's passionate quest for inebriation through wine in his provocative *Intoxication: Life in Pursuit of Artificial Paradise* (New York: E. P. Dutton, 1989).
3. Edward S. Hyams, *Dionysus: A Social History of the Wine Vine* (New York: Macmillan, 1965), 7.
4. See Hyams's discussion, in *Dionysus*, 7–8, of physiological, economic, and religious reasons that wine, among all intoxicants, became so culturally widespread.
5. See Bruce Lincoln's article, "Beverages," in *The Encyclopedia of Religion*, 16 vols. (New York: Macmillan Publishing Co., 1987), 2: 119–23.
6. Ibid., 2: 121.
7. W. K. C. Guthrie, *The Greeks and Their Gods* (Boston: Beacon Press, 1950), 174. See also Charles Seltman, *Wine in the Ancient World* (London: Routledge and Kegan Paul, 1957), and Henry F. Lutz, *Viticulture and Brewing in the Ancient Orient* (New York: G. E. Stechert, 1922).
8. See the lengthy discussion of wine ("Khamr") in H. A. R. Gibb and J. H. Kramers, *Shorter Encyclopedia of Islam* (Leiden: E. J. Brill, 1953), 243–45.
9. Johnson, *World Atlas of Wine*, 174.

10. See Desmond Seward, *Monks and Wine* (New York: Crown Publishers, 1983).
11. Selden Bacon's seminal writings in the 1940s focused interest on studying the social and cultural contexts of drinking behaviors. Helpful introductions to the research conducted in this field over the past six decades include Dwight B. Heath, "Anthropological Perspectives on Alcohol: A Historical Review," in *Cross-Cultural Approaches to the Study of Alcohol,* Michael Everett, Jack Waddell, and Dwight Heath, eds. (The Hague: Mouton Publishers, 1976), 45–107; Kaye Middleton Fillmore, "Competing Paradigms in Biomedical and Social Science Alcohol Research: The 1940s Through the 1980s," in *Alcohol: The Development of Sociological Perspectives on Use and Abuse,* Paul Roman, ed. (New Brunswick, N.J.: Rutgers Center of Alcohol Studies, 1991), 59–86; and Harry Levine, "The Promise and Problems of Alcohol Sociology," in *Alcohol: The Development of Sociological Perspectives,* 87–112.
12. Claude Levi-Strauss, *The Origin of Table Manners* (New York: Harper and Row, 1979), 495.

1. Religion, Wine, and Eastern "High Culture"

1. Thomas Pinney, *A History of Wine in America* (Berkeley: University of California Press, 1989), contains a helpful account of the "Ericsson Wineland" legend. Pinney notes that "the latest opinion inclines to the belief that the vines of Leif Ericsson's 'Wineland'—most probably the northern coast of Newfoundland— were in fact not grapes at all but the plants of the wild cranberry. Another guess is that what the Vikings named the land for was meadow grass, called archaically *vin* or *vinber,* and misinterpreted by later tellers of the saga" (3).
2. In their *American Vines* (New York: Duell, Sloan, and Pearce, 1951), Frank Schoonmaker and Tom Marvel write that Lord Delaware prompted the first attempt at growing vinifera grapes by writing the London Company in 1616 that "[i]n every boske and hedge, and not farr from our pallisade gates we have thousands of goodly vines running along and leaving to every tree, which yields a plentiful grape in their kind. Let me appeal, then, to knowledge if these naturall vines were planted, dressed and ordered by skilful vinearoons, whether we might not make a perfect grape and fruitful vintage in short time?" In 1619 the London Company finally sent a group of French vinticulturists to plant and cultivate vines from both France and Germany. It might also be noted that in 1619 the general assembly of Virginia passed an act that required every land-owner to plant vines and seek out instruction on their proper cultivation. This attempt to encourage American wine production, aided partly by an incentive of servants to be given to those who undertook large plantings, succeeded in stimulating the planting of thousands of vines.
3. In his *A History of Wine in America,* Thomas Pinney notes that the principal source from which our notion of the original Thanksgiving is derived, Edward Winslow's letter of Dec. 11, 1621, makes no reference to wine being served at the meal (29). Nonetheless, many historians have perpetuated the belief that wine was present at the first Thanksgiving, and, owing to the settlers' fondness for wine, it is possible that newly made wine was available.

4. Emil Oberholzer, *Delinquent Saints: Disciplinary Action in the Early Congregational Churches of Massachusetts* (New York: Columbia University Press, 1956), 152.

5. Increase Mather, *Wo to Drunkards,* cited in W. J. Rorabaugh, *The Alcoholic Republic* (New York: Oxford Press, 1979), 30.

6. Ibid.

7. William Penn, cited in Pinney, *A History of Wine in America,* 32.

8. See Ulysses P. Hendrick, *The Grapes of New York, Fifteenth Report of the New York Agricultural Experiment Station for the Year 1907* (Albany: J. B. Lyon, State Printer, 1907), 7–9.

9. A thorough discussion of the Huguenots' contributions to American wine making can be found in Pinney, *A History of Wine in America,* 30–32, 36–37, and 100–102.

10. Ibid., 62.

11. Ralph Waldo Emerson, cited in *The Fireside Book of Wine: An Anthology for Wine Drinkers,* Alexis Bespaloff, ed. (New York: Simon and Schuster, 1977), 40. Apparently, Emerson's colleague, Henry David Thoreau, did not find the same intrinsic value in wine, as in *Walden* he averred, "I believe that water is the only drink for a wise man; wine is not so noble a liquor; and think of dashing the hopes of a morning with a cup of warm coffee, or of an evening with a dish of tea! Ah, how low I fall when I am tempted by them! Even music may be intoxicating. Such apparently slight causes destroyed Greece and Rome, and will destroy England and America" (*Fireside Book,* 218).

12. Statistical summaries of Americans' consumption of wine, beer, cider, and distilled spirits can be found in appendix 1 of Rorabaugh, *Alcoholic Republic.*

13. Ibid., 173.

14. Ibid., 174.

15. Benjamin Franklin, cited in *Fireside Book of Wine,* 219.

16. Benjamin Franklin, cited in J. C. Furnas, *The Life and Times of the Late Demon Rum* (New York: Capricorn Books, 1973), 17.

17. Benjamin Franklin, cited in *Fireside Book of Wine,* 219.

18. An entertaining account of Franklin's interest in wine is to be found in Claude-Anne Lopez, *Mon Cher Papa: Franklin and the Ladies of Paris* (New Haven: Yale University Press, 1966), 290–96.

19. Benjamin Franklin, cited in *Fireside Book of Wine,* 220.

20. Benjamin Franklin, cited in *Benjamin Franklin: Representative Selections,* Frank L. Mott and Chester E. Jorgenson, eds. (New York: American Book Co., 1936), 69–70.

21. Thomas Jefferson, cited in Adams, *Wines of America,* 18. Of anecdotal interest is the fact that a cache of bottles was discovered in the early 1980s in an old bricked-up cellar in the Marias district of Paris containing a group of bottles with the letters "Th.J." etched on their sides. It was assumed that these wines had been ordered by Thomas Jefferson, but for some unknown reason were never shipped. The "Jefferson wines" included more than a dozen bottles of Lafite, Yquem, Margaux, and Mouton from the 1784 and 1787 vintages. The famed wine collector Hardy Rodenstock of West Germany purchased these

wines and later sold some through Christie's wine auction in London. Christopher Forbes, son of publishing magnate Malcolm Forbes, paid $156,450 for the 1787 "Jefferson" Lafite. A 1784 Yquem with the Jefferson initials sold for $56,000. There is, of course, little way of verifying the authenticity of these bottles as having been owned (but never possessed) by Jefferson. Although most of Jefferson's wine purchases were recorded, researchers at Jefferson's estate at Monticello have been unable to find records showing that Jefferson bought any wine from the 1787 vintage.

22. John F. Kennedy, cited in *The Little, Brown Book of Anecdotes*, Clifton Fadiman, ed. (Boston: Little, Brown and Company, 1985), 328.

23. It might be noted that Richard Nixon created a worldwide reputation for Schramsberg Vineyard's sparkling wines by bringing them with him to toast Chairman Mao on his famed trip to reestablish diplomatic relations with China. Nixon was an unabashed lover of fine French Bordeaux, and he apparently had little affection for his home state's wine, which he virtually banned from being served at White House state dinners. See *From the President: Richard Nixon's Secret Files* (New York: Harper and Row, 1989). It has been reported that Nixon so loved 1966 Chateau Margaux that he ordered his stewards to serve it to him wrapped in a towel while pouring his guests a six-dollar wine. See Bob Woodward and Carl Bernstein, *The Final Days* (New York: Simon and Schuster, 1976), 238. Another president, Andrew Jackson, was likewise a wine buff. Introduced to the subtleties and pleasures of the wine stored in Aaron Burr's impressive cellar, Jackson subsequently stocked the Hermitage in Tennessee with a selection that led to its reputation as the wine center of the West. See Rorabaugh, *Alcoholic Republic*, 102–3. In more recent years Gerald Ford helped publicize Michigan wines, such as Tabor Hill, during his White House years, and Ronald Reagan drew upon his aide Michael Deaver's wine expertise to serve a consistently superb array of California's best wines.

24. Jefferson was, without doubt, one of the foremost "secular humanists" in American history. By no means an atheist, he favored what is generally referred to as deism, an Enlightenment philosophy that seeks to interject rationalism into the Western religious tradition. Readers might wish to consult Jefferson, *The Life and Morals of Jesus of Nazareth, Extracted Textually From the Gospels of Matthew, Mark, Luke, and John* (Boston: Beacon Press, 1951).

25. Thomas Jefferson, *The Writings of Thomas Jefferson*, Andrew A. Lipscomb, ed. (Washington, D.C.: The Thomas Jefferson Memorial Association, 1903), 15: 492.

26. Cited in Daniel Boorstin, *The Lost World of Thomas Jefferson* (Boston: Beacon Press, 1960), 706–7.

27. Rorabaugh's *Alcoholic Republic* clearly substantiates this connection between wine and "highbrow culture." His historical narrative demonstrates the tendency of "gentlemen who by reason of their wealth, prestige, and popularity" preferred expensive, imported wines to cheap, domestic rum or whiskey. Officeholders, however, often were embarrassed by the "unpatriotic" nature of their preferred beverage and so at least occasionally disassociated themselves from this imported luxury item. Rorabaugh cites the records of a candidate for

political office whose ledger shows the purchase of over eighty gallons of whiskey to declare himself a candidate to the general populace and "ten bottles of wine at different times among merchants for the purpose of shewing [*sic*] that I was a gentleman and fond of the importation of foreign luxuries" (154).

28. Selden Bacon, "Alcohol and Complex Society," reprinted in *Society, Culture and Drinking Patterns*, David Pittman and Charles Snyder, eds. (New York: John Wiley and Sons, 1962), 78–93.

29. Donald Horton, "The Function of Alcohol in Primitive Societies: A Cross-Cultural Study," *Quarterly Journal for the Study of Alcohol* 4 (1943): 199–320.

30. The importance of "critical interpretation" in the wine-tasting experience is carefully described in Ray Brady, "Secrets of Wine Tasting," Maynard Amerine, "Sensory Evaluation, or How to Taste Wine," and William Fretter, "Wine as Art," in *The University of California/Sotheby Book*.

2. Western Expansion: Religion and "A Happy Wineland"

1. Readers interested in the history of California wines might wish to consult *Early History of Wine Production in California* (San Francisco: Wine Institute, 1941); Vincent Carosso, "The Commercial Development of California Vinticulture" (Ph.D. diss., University of California, 1949); Theodore Schoenman, ed., *Father of California Wine: Agoston Haraszthy* (Santa Barbara: Capra Press, 1979); and William Cruess, *A Half Century in Food and Wine Technology* (Berkeley: University of California Oral History Office, 1967).

2. A helpful overview of canon law concerning wine making and the development of altar wine in the United States can be found in Thomas D. Terry, S.J., "Altar Wines," in *The University of California/Sotheby Book*, 297–301.

3. There is little question but that Father Juniper Serra deserves the primary credit for the cultivation of the vinifera species in Alta California. It was Gen. Mariano Guadalupe Vallejo who, on the basis of his father's memories of conversations with Serra, originated this account. Historians have come to think that the story is not quite this simple, however, as can be learned by reading Ray Brady, "Alta California's First Vintage," in *The University of California/ Sotheby Book*, 10–15.

4. In addition to Ray Brady's article, "Alta California's First Vintage," readers might wish to consult the discussion of early California missions in Pinney, *A History of Wine in America*, 233–43.

5. Pinney, *A History of Wine in America*, 240–41.

6. Helpful accounts of the role of immigrants in the American wine industry can be found in Jack Chen, "The Contributions of the Chinese," and Eileen Hayes, "Those Who Worked the Land," in *The University of California/Sotheby Book*.

7. Fredrich Muench, *School for American Grape Culture* (St. Louis: Conrad Witter, 1865), 11. Muench also wrote that "[t]he people in the wine countries are gay, lively and impulsive, social, liberal and temperate, very different from the beer consumers or gin drinkers" (134).

8. A copy of Frederick Muench, *Religion and Christianity* (Hermann: Muehl and Strehly, 1843), is in the collection at the Missouri Historical Society.

9. Ibid., 10.

10. Ibid., 5.

11. Ibid., 10, 34.

12. I am grateful for the assistance of Linda Walker Stevens for much of the following material on George Husmann. A writer and editor living in Hermann, Missouri, Linda Stevens has been researching the German wine makers of the region for a decade.

13. George Husman, "The Knowledge of Plant Life: An Important Factor in Education," *14th Annual Report of the Missouri State Board of Agriculture for 1879* (Jefferson City, 1880), 24.

14. Charles Nordhoff, *The Communistic Societies of the United States* (1875; reprint, New York: Schocken Books, 1970).

15. Readers might wish to consult William R. Perkins and Barthnius L. Lick, *History of the Amana Society* (1891; reprint, New York: Arno Press, 1975), and Bertha Shambaugh, *Amana That Was and Amana That Is* (Iowa City: Historical Society of Iowa, 1932).

16. George Kraus (as told to E. Mae Fritz), *The Story of an Amana Winemaker* (Iowa City: Penfield Press, 1984), 100.

17. Ibid. Most of the material in this section is drawn from Mr. Kraus's account of wine making in Old Amana.

18. Ibid., 45.

19. Mary Douglas, "On Deciphering a Meal," in *Implicit Meanings* (London: Routledge and Kegan Paul, 1975), 260.

20. Ibid.

21. See Pinney, *A History of Wine in America*, 131.

22. George Husmann, cited in Adams, *Wines of America*, 168.

3. Wine and American Religious Communities

1. See E. O. Wilson's discussion of how biologically rooted concepts such as tribalism, territorialism, and boundary posturing explain human group behavior in *Sociobiology: The New Synthesis* (Cambridge, Mass.: Belknap Press, 1975), 564–65.

2. For a discussion of the cultural dominance of mainstream Protestantism, Catholicism, and Judaism, see Will Herberg's classic study, *Protestant, Catholic, Jew: An Essay in American Religious Sociology* (Garden City, N.Y.: Doubleday and Co., 1955).

3. A reliable reference on religious and cultural institutions of ancient Israel is Roland de Vaux, *Ancient Israel* (New York: McGraw-Hill, 1965). Readers might also wish to consult the entry on wine in *Encyclopedia Judaica* (Jerusalem: Keter Publishers, 1971). Sources that describe the use of wine in contemporary Jewish life are Rabbi Hayim Halvey Donin's books, *To Be a Jew: A Guide to Jewish Observance in Contemporary Life* (New York: Basic Books, 1977) and *To*

Pray as a Jew (New York: Basic Books, 1980), and Rabbi Gersion Appel, *The Concise Code of Jewish Law* (New York: Yeshiva University Press, 1977).

4. A more thorough description of the prescriptions governing the use of wine in Jewish religious observances can be found in Charles Snyder, *Alcohol and the Jews: A Cultural Study of Drinking and Sobriety* (Glencoe, Ill.: Free Press, 1958), 19–34.

5. Robert F. Bales, "The 'Fixation Factor' in Alcohol Addiction: An Hypothesis Derived from a Comparative Study of Irish and Jewish Social Norms," cited in Snyder, *Alcohol and the Jews*, 21.

6. Robert F. Bales, cited in Snyder, *Alcohol and the Jews*, 34.

7. See Mary Douglas, *Purity and Danger* (New York: Penguin Books, 1970), and "Pollution," in her *Implicit Meanings*, 47–59.

8. *The Jewish Dietary Law* (New York: The Rabbinical Assembly of America, 1982), 73.

9. Appel, *Concise Code of Jewish Law*, 274.

10. Leon Adams, "The Kosher Winemakers," in *The Wines of America* (New York: McGraw-Hill Book Company, 1973), 488–91.

11. Ibid., 489.

12. Mark Keller, "The Great Jewish Drink Mystery," *British Journal of Addiction* 64 (1970): 294.

13. Robert F. Bales, "Cultural Differences in Rates of Alcoholism," *Quarterly Journal for the Study of Alcohol* 6 (1946): 480–99.

14. Snyder, *Alcohol and the Jews*, and "Culture and Jewish Sobriety," in *Society, Culture, and Drinking Patterns*, David Pittman and Charles Snyder, eds. (New York: John Wiley and Sons, 1962), 188–225.

15. See Harold Y. Vaderpool's discussion of Methodism's health and moral codes in "The Wesleyan-Methodist Tradition," in *Caring and Curing: Health and Medicine in the Western Religious Traditions*, Ronald L. Numbers and Darrel W. Amundsen, eds. (New York: Macmillan Publishing Co., 1986), 326.

16. Ibid., 341.

17. See Timothy Weber's discussion of Baptists' health and moral codes in "The Baptist Tradition," in *Caring and Curing*, 297.

18. Ibid.

19. See David Edwin Harrell Jr.'s discussion of the Disciples of Christ's health and moral codes in "The Disciples of Christ-Church of Christ Tradition," in *Caring and Curing*, 376–96.

20. James H. Garrison, cited in Harrell's "The Disciples of Christ-Church of Christ Tradition," 384.

21. See Sydney Ahlstrom's discussion of the "sectarian impulse" in *A Religious History of the American People* (New Haven: Yale University Press, 1972), 472–90, and Winthrop Hudson, *Religion in America* (New York: Charles Scribner's Sons, 1981), 182–205.

22. A discussion of the way in which members of "intentional communities" became committed to a natural or primitive way of life that "links strong views about sex, possessions, and bodily intake" can be found in Laurence Veysey, *The Communal Experience* (New York: Harper and Row, 1973).

23. I am indebted here to Lawrence Foster's volume, *Religion and Sexuality: The Shakers, the Mormons and the Oneida Community* (Champaign: University of Illinois Press, 1984).

24. *Doctrine and Covenants*, Section 32, 2.

25. Ibid., Section 27, 3–4. Many Mormons interpret the word "new" to mean unfermented grape juice.

26. Ibid., Section 27, 5.

27. Ibid., Section 89, 5–6.

28. Joseph Smith, *History of the Church of Jesus Christ of Latter-Day Saints, Period 1, History of Joseph Smith, the Prophet, By Himself,* 5 vols. (Salt Lake City: Desert, 1954), 2: 369.

29. Ibid., 378.

30. Ibid., 446.

31. LaMar Petersen, *Hearts Made Glad: The Charges of Intemperance Against Joseph Smith the Mormon Prophet* (Salt Lake City: n.p., 1975), 167.

32. Ibid., 84.

33. Oliver Huntington, cited in Petersen, *Hearts Made Glad,* 156.

34. Diary entries of Apr. 23 and Apr. 29, 1846, by Samuel Richards, cited in Petersen, *Hearts Made Glad,* 200.

35. Brigham Young, cited in Leonard Arrington, "An Economic Interpretation of the Word of Wisdom," *Brigham Young University Studies* (1959): 46. LaMar Petersen cites the diary entry of John D. Lee, who visited Brigham on May 15, 1867: "On the following day I went to see him in his Mansion where I spent near 1/2 day—verry agreeable indeed. He had a Decanter of Splendid Wine brought in of his own make & said, I want to treat Bro. Lee to as Good an article, I think, as can be bought in Dixie. The wine indeed was a Superior article. He said that he had some 300 gallons & treated about 2000$ worth of Liqueurs yearly & continued that we [he] wished that some one would take his wine at 5$ Per gallon & sell it, where upon Pres. D. H. Wells Said that he would take 200 gals. at 6$ a gallon &c. The Pres. told me that [he] Staid over night at my House in Washing[ton] & that he enjoyed himself well & that Bro. Jas. Pace was there & felt well &c." (*Hearts Made Glad,* 156).

36. Arrington, "An Economic Interpretation," 47.

37. Leonard Arrington's article provides a convincing argument that the Word of Wisdom functioned to help the Latter Day Saints in Utah achieve economic self-sufficiency. Further interpretation of the cultural setting in which Joseph Smith received the Word of Wisdom can be found in Thomas G. Alexander, *Mormonism in Transition. A History of the Latter-Day Saints, 1890–1930* (Urbana: University of Illinois Press, 1986), 258–71.

38. See R. Laurence Moore, "Insiders and Outsiders in American Historical Narrative and American History," *The American Historical Review* 87 (1982): 390–412.

39. See Victor Turner, *The Ritual Process* (Ithaca: Cornell University Press, 1969), 131–40.

40. See Ronald L. Numbers and David R. Larson, "The Adventist Tradition," in *Caring and Curing,* 449.

41. William James, *The Varieties of Religious Experience* (Cambridge: Harvard University Press, 1985), 19.
42. Thomas Lake Harris, quoted in R. Laurence Moore, *In Search of White Crows* (New York: Oxford University Press, 1977), 12.
43. For discussions of Thomas Lake Harris's role in both American religious thought and in American popular psychology, see Robert C. Fuller, *Mesmerism and the American Cure of Souls* (Philadelphia: University of Pennsylvania Press, 1982), and Fuller, *Americans and the Unconscious* (New York: Oxford University Press, 1986).
44. Thomas Lake Harris, quoted in Moore, *In Search of White Crows*, 18.
45. Thomas Lake Harris, quoted in Herbert Schneider and George Lawton, *A Prophet and a Pilgrim* (New York: Columbia University Press, 1942), 160.
46. Thomas Lake Harris, quoted in Adams, *Wines of America*, 142.
47. Schneider and Lawton, *A Prophet and a Pilgrim*, 167.
48. See Adams, *The Wines of America*, 150–52, and Pinney, *A History of Wine in America*, 332–35.
49. The following information is contained in a pamphlet published by Summum entitled *The First Encounter*.
50. The basic beliefs and practices of Summum are contained in Summum Bonum Amen Ra's *SUMMUM: Sealed Except to the Open Mind* (Salt Lake City: Summum, 1988).
51. From a Summum pamphlet entitled *Nectar of the Gods*.

4. The Grapes of Wrath: Prohibition

1. An engaging, if brief, account of the Pilgrim's "beer crisis" can be found in Mark Lender and James Martin, *Drinking in America* (New York: Free Press, 1982), 2–3.
2. Ibid., 2.
3. Daniel Dorchester, *Christianity in the United States* (New York: Phillips and Hunt, 1888).
4. See Lender and Martin, *Drinking in America*, 12.
5. Daniel Dorchester, cited in Lender and Martin, *Drinking in America*, 12.
6. Daniel Dorchester, *The Liquor Problem In All Ages* (New York: Phillips and Hunt, 1884), 125. Dorchester's account goes on to record that "[t]owns provided intoxicating drinks at the funerals of their paupers. In Salem, in 1728, at the funeral of a pauper, a gallon of wine and another of cider are charged as 'incidentals'; the next year six gallons of wine on a similar occasion. In Lynn, in 1711, the town furnished 'half a barrel of cider for the widow Dispaw's funeral.' Affairs came to such a pass that, in 1742, the General Court of Massachusetts forbid the use of wine and rum at funerals."
7. J. C. Furnas, *The Life and Times of the Late Demon Rum*, 9.
8. Lyman Beecher, *The Autobiography of Lyman Beecher*, Barbara M. Cross, ed., 2 vols. (Cambridge, Mass.: Belknap Press, 1961), 1: 179–84. Describing how a recent ordination ceremony "looked and smelled like the bar of a very active grog-shop," Beecher bemoaned: "When they had all done drinking, and had

taken pipes and tobacco, in less than fifteen minutes there was such a smoke you couldn't see. And the noise I can not describe; it was the maximum of hilarity. They told their stories, and were at the height of jocose talk. They were not old-fashioned Puritans. They had been run down. Great deal of spirituality on Sabbath, and not much when they got where there was something good to drink" (1: 179).

9. Lender and Martin, *Drinking in America*, 54.

10. In *The Dry Years: Prohibition and Social Change in Washington* (Seattle: University of Washington Press, 1965), Norman Clark argues:

> [T]here is a broad period in American history which might be called the 'Age of Evangelism,' a period during which evangelism as a quality of life permeated individual and social being. Its components would be romantic optimism, strong emotionalism, passions for righteousness, and convictions that righteousness could be grasped through vigorous action; hence the pledges, the parades, the speeches, the songs, the votes. This quality tapped what Reinhold Niebuhr calls the "deep layer of Messianic consciousness in the mind of America." It included also a demand for maximum dedication and efficiency, an eagerness to sacrifice, and a sense of moral uplift in the sacrifices of others. There was a color here, to be sure, that approached the discomforting shades of fanaticism, and one could easily identify in this period a good number of fanatics in the ranks of evangelical religion, politics, unionism, or technology.
>
> The evangelical character of the prohibition movement expressed the qualities very well. Though it was imbued with selfish economic motives, class tensions, maybe even with subconscious racial and sexual fears—with paranoia, stupidity, and greed—the prohibition movement also urged men and women to vote with their hearts and with their sometimes desperate hope that they could restore the lost purity of the great agrarian dream and make a better world. (126–27)

11. Rorabaugh, *Alcoholic Republic*, 210.

12. Jefferson, *The Writings of Thomas Jefferson*, 15: 177.

13. Charles Nordhoff, *The Communistic Societies of the United States* (1875; reprint, New York: Schocken Books, 1970), 403.

14. Dorchester, *Liquor Problem*, 260.

15. Ibid.

16. Ibid., 264.

17. See Mary Douglas, *Purity and Danger* (New York: Penguin Books, 1970), 18.

18. Dorchester, *Liquor Problem*, 24–30. Dorchester cites two clergymen from California to help support his contention that "evidence from the vine-growing portions of the United States does not favor the theory that the free use of native wines would promote temperance" (see 569–70). Not every temperance advocate agreed with Dorchester's line of reasoning, however. The Massachusetts Temperance Society published a volume entitled *When Will the Day Come?* (Boston: John Wilson and Son, 1857) that notes how members rose at an orga-

nizational meeting and cited the relationship between wine drinking and temperance en route to defeating a resolution that sought to add wine to the list of prohibited beverages. The Massachusetts Temperance Society apparently did, however, feel free to dismiss the relevance of biblical uses of wine on the grounds that "wines" in the United States were "spurious compounds, without grape-juice" and "aggravated by poisonous adulterations" (175–76).

19. One of the foremost church historians of the nineteenth century was Robert Baird. In his evangelically biased classic work, *Religion in the United States of America* (1864; reprint, New York: Arno Press, 1969), he writes:

> To reach the poor as well as to remove temptation from the rich, the rules of the temperance societies within the last six or seven years have included "all intoxicating drinks." Upon this principle wines of all descriptions have generally been abandoned, both on account of their being generally impure with us—being imported, and all more or less intoxicating, and because they are not found necessary to persons in health, but on the contrary, injurious, besides which, it was of consequence that an example should be given by those who could afford to buy wine to the poor who could not. (389)

20. *Temperance Recorder,* Apr. 1835, cited in John Allen Krout, *The Origins of Prohibition* (New York: Knopf, 1925), 158.

21. Biographical accounts of Thomas and Charles Welch can be found in William Chazanof, *Welch's Grape Juice* (Syracuse: Syracuse University Press, 1977). This quotation comes from page 1.

22. Oliver Wendell Holmes, *The Autocrat of the Breakfast Table* (Boston: Houghton, Mifflin and Company, 1858), 48.

23. James H. Timberlake, *Prohibition and the Progressive Movement, 1900–1920* (Cambridge: Harvard University Press, 1966).

24. A helpful overview of the effect of Prohibition upon the wine industry can be found in Ruth Teiser and Catherine Harroun, "Volstead Act, Rebirth, and Boom," in *The University of California/Sotheby Book,* 50–81.

25. Quoted in Teiser and Harroun, "Volstead Act, Rebirth, and Boom," 54.

5. Popular Religion and the Wine Revolution

1. Kirby Moulton, "The Economics of Wine in California," in *The University of California/Sotheby Book,* 380–405. Note that the per capita wine consumption in both France and Italy is twenty-five gallons annually; Argentina averages twenty gallons; Spain averages seventeen; the Soviet Union averages about four; and the United Kingdom averages about two. The 2.3 gallons of wine per capita drunk in the United States each year compares to thirty-nine gallons of soft drinks, thirty-seven gallons of beer, and twenty-eight gallons of milk.

2. See Carol Spivack and Richard Weinstock, *Gourmet Food and Wine Festivals of North America* (Ventura, Calif.: Printwheel Press, 1986).

3. See John Bender, "Tasting Groups," and Paul Schulten, "Social Organizations," in *The University of California/Sotheby Book.*

4. Bender, "Tasting Groups," 354.

5. Robert Parker's *The Wine Advocate* is one of the best-known periodicals that specializes in tasting results and comparative ratings. Hugh Johnson, *Pocket Encyclopedia of Wine* (New York: Simon and Schuster), and Michael Broadbent, *Pocket Guide to Wine Tasting* (New York: Simon and Schuster, 1982), are fine examples of "how-to-buy-and-drink" books. *The Wine Spectator* is perhaps the best-known wine periodical.

6. H. Warner Allen, *The Romance of Wine* (New York: E. P. Dutton and Co., 1932), 15.

7. See Adrienne Lehrer's fine study of the lexical meanings and semantic structures of "wine talk" in *Wine and Conversation* (Bloomington: Indiana University Press, 1983).

8. Citation from the Mishnah, quoted in Elliot N. Dorff, "The Jewish Tradition," in *Caring and Curing*, 20.

9. E. A. Maury, *Wine Is the Best Medicine* (Kansas City: Sheed Andrews and McMeel, 1974); Marjorie Michaels, *Stay Healthy with Wine* (New York: Dial Press, 1981); Salvatore Lucia, *A History of Wine as Therapy* (Philadelphia: Lippincott, 1963). See also William Dickerson, "Medical and Therapeutic Values," in *The University of California/Sotheby Book*, 368–80, and Gene Ford, *The Benefits of Moderate Drinking* (San Francisco: Wine Appreciation Guild, 1981).

10. David Whitten and Martin Lipp, *To Your Health!* (New York: HarperCollins, 1994). Whitten and Lipp provide a fourteen-page bibliography of published materials, largely drawn from academic and medical journals, that assess the effect of wine drinking on various measures of human health. See also Lewis Perdue, *The French Paradox and Beyond* (Sonoma, Calif.: Renaissance Publishing, 1992).

11. See *Wine and the Artist* (New York: Dover Publications, 1979).

12. See David Goines, Adrian Wilson, and Andrew Hayem, "The Art of the Label," and Roy Brady, "Collecting Wine Labels," in *The University of California/Sotheby Book*. For example, the Mondavi winery—pictured on most Mondavi labels—is built in the style of California missions and thus associates this religiocultural heritage with its fine wines. The Jordan winery, also depicted on its labels, is an almost slavish imitation of French chateaux. Of further interest is the marvelously camp "Marilyn Merlot" label, depicting a voluptuous picture of Marilyn Monroe on Merlot Napa Valley's 1986 release. Comedian-winemaker Pat Paulsen's "Refrigerator Red" or almost any of Bully Hill's labels also exemplifies the somewhat slapstick character of much American wine art. And, too, for $19.95, wine connoisseurs can buy a videocassette of Pat Paulsen's deadpan routine entitled "Three Cheers for the Red, White, and Rosé."

13. See Catherine Albanese's chapter on cultural religion in *America: Religions and Religion* (Belmont, Calif.: Wadsworth Publishing Co., 1981), 311–44, and Peter Williams, *Popular Religion in America* (Englewood Cliffs, N.J.: Prentice-Hall, 1980).

14. See Gen. 27:28; Deut. 7:13; Amos 9:14.

15. See Amos 9:13; Joel 3:18; Zech. 9:17.

16. For example, in Eccl. 9:7 we are told to "Go, eat your bread with enjoyment and drink your wine with a merry heart." Eccl. 10:19 counsels that "wine gladdens life." Ps. 104:15 rejoices in God's manifold works and praises God for making "wine to gladden the heart of man." Zech. 10:17 promises that when God answers our prayers our "hearts shall be glad as with wine."

17. Rabbi Leo Trapp, cited in Thomas Terry, "Altar Wines," in *The University of California/Sotheby Book,* 297.

18. Allen, *The Romance of Wine,* 18.

19. See Victor Turner, *The Ritual Process* (Ithaca, N.Y.: Cornell University Press, 1977).

20. George Saintsbury, *Notes on a Cellar-Book* (New York: Macmillan Co., 1933), xvii. Although both Saintsbury's and H. Warner Allen's books were originally intended for British audiences, their wide distribution in the United States justifies their inclusion in this cultural history.

21. Charles Senn Taylor, "Prolegomena to an Aesthetics of Wine," *The Journal of Speculative Philosophy* 2 (1988): 132.

22. Catherine Albanese, *Nature Religion in America* (Chicago: University of Chicago Press, 1990).

23. James, *The Varieties of Religious Experience,* 307.

24. Ibid.

25. William James, "Subjective Effects of Nitrous Oxide," *Mind* 7 (1882): 186.

Epilogue. Religion and Wine: Concluding Observations

1. Lincoln, "Beverages," 119.

2. Ibid., 120.

3. Turner, *The Ritual Process,* 97.

4. Douglas, *Implicit Meanings,* 260.

5. Lincoln, "Beverages," 120. See also D. T. Suzuki, *Zen and Japanese Culture* (Princeton: Princeton University Press, 1970), and Theodore M. Ludwig, "The Way of Tea: A Religio-Aesthetic Mode of Life," *History of Religions* 14 (1970): 28–50.

6. James, *The Varieties of Religious Experience,* 307.

7. Turner, *The Ritual Process,* 106.

8. Ralph Waldo Emerson, *The Complete Works of Ralph Waldo Emerson,* 12 vols. (New York: AMS Press, 1968), 1: 62.

9. See Douglas, *Purity and Danger,* 18.

Suggested Readings

There are several reliable reference volumes that would provide excellent beginning points for further studies of the cultural history of wine in the United States. Among the best of these are Leon Adams, *The Wines of America* (New York: McGraw-Hill Book Co., 1990), and Thomas Pinney, *A History of Wine in America* (Berkeley: University of California Press, 1989). Both offer sound historical surveys of the development of wine production in the United States from precolonial times to the present. The approximately fifty essays appearing in Doris Muscatine, Maynard Amerine, and Bob Thompson, eds., *The University of California/Sotheby Book of California Wine* (Berkeley: University of California Press/Sotheby Publications, 1984), are invaluable aids to the wider cultural contexts of the production and consumption of wine. Although limited to the history of California wine, these essays treat such topics as the role of the early Franciscans, the gold rush era, the contributions of immigrants, the effect of Prohibition, altar wines, the medical values of wine, and the "sociology" of wine-tasting groups. Treatments of the religious and cultural history of wine in earlier eras of human history can be found in Desmond Seward, *Monks and Wine* (New York: Crown Publishers, 1983), Edward Hyams, *Dionysus: A Social History of the Wine Vine* (New York: Macmillan, 1965), and Charles Seltman, *Wine in the Ancient World* (London: Routledge and Kegan Paul, 1957). Two classics in the literature describing the "subjective romance" elicited by wine drinking are George Saintsbury, *Notes on a Cellar-Book* (New York: Macmillan Co., 1933), and Herbert Warner Allen, *The Romance of Wine* (New York: E. P. Dutton and Co., 1933). Readers less interested in the cultural history of wine might wish to consult standard reference books that discuss the role of climate, soil, and technology in wine making, such as Hugh Johnson, *The World Atlas of Wine* (New York: Simon and Schuster, 1985), Andre Simon, ed., *Wines of the World* (New York: McGraw-Hill Publishing, 1972), or

Anthony Dias Blue, *American Wine: A Comprehensive Guide* (New York: Harper and Row, 1988).

A great deal of literature exists on the anthropological and sociological study of alcohol use, although there is relatively little written on the use of wine per se. Readers might wish to begin with Dwight B. Heath's essay, "Anthropological Perspectives on Alcohol: A Historical Review," as well as the other articles in Michael Everett, Jack Waddell, and Dwight Heath, eds., *Cross-Cultural Approaches to the Study of Alcohol* (The Hague: Mouton Publishers, 1976). The articles in David Pittman and Charles Snyder, eds., *Society, Culture, and Drinking Patterns* (New York: John Wiley and Sons, 1962), are helpful introductions to the cultural study of alcohol consumption, particularly Selden Bacon's 1944 study, "Alcohol and Complex Society," which helped direct researchers' attention to the need for more sophisticated understandings of the ways in which cultures shape drinking patterns. Although it appears that most social scientific studies of alcohol consumption have been conducted with the intention of helping to understand the roots of pathological drinking, some researchers have followed Bacon's call for a more comprehensive view of the cultural forces that shape drinking behaviors, and some of their findings can be found in Paul Roman, ed., *Alcohol: The Development of Sociological Perspectives on Use and Abuse* (New Brunswick, N.J.: Rutgers Center of Alcohol Studies, 1991). Additional perspectives on the cultural settings that influence attitudes toward alcohol consumption can be found in the lively historical narratives of W. J. Rorabaugh, *The Alcoholic Republic* (New York: Oxford University Press, 1979), and J. C. Furnas, *The Life and Times of the Late Demon Rum* (New York: Capricorn Books, 1973).

A fascinating topic for further study is the role of wine in eliciting altered states of consciousness that facilitate aesthetic and mystical experiences. Ronald Siegel, *Intoxication: Life in Pursuit of Artificial Paradise* (New York: E. P. Dutton, 1989), provides a great deal of insight into humanity's age-old quest for inebriation. Additional perspectives on the role that alcohol has had in producing aesthetic and mystical states of consciousness can be found in Charles Tart, ed., *Altered States of Consciousness* (Garden City, N.Y.: Anchor Books, 1969). Religions, of course, have long used intoxicating beverages as a means of eliciting particular forms of experience. An overview of the role that intoxicating beverages have had in world religions can be found in Bruce Lincoln's essay, "Beverages," in *The Encyclopedia of Religion*, 16 vols. (New York: Macmillan, 1987), 2: 119-23. Excellent examples of the scholarly investigation of the ways in which alcoholic beverages elicit religious experience are Lawrence E. Sullivan, *Icanchu's Drum* (New

York: Macmillan, 1988), Gerardo Reichel-Dolmatoff, *The Shaman and the Jaguar* (Philadelphia: Temple University Press, 1975), and Herman Lommel, "Konig Soma," *Numen* 2 (1955): 196–205.

Further understandings of "unchurched" forms of American religious life can be found in Peter Williams, *Popular Religion in America* (Englewood Cliffs, N.J.: Prentice Hall, 1980) and Catherine Albanese, *Nature Religion in America* (Chicago: University of Chicago Press, 1990), and her chapter on cultural religion in *America: Religions and Religion* (Belmont, Calif.: Wadsworth Publishing Co. 1981). Charles Senn Taylor, "Prolegomena to an Aesthetics of Wine," *The Journal of Speculative Philosophy* 2 (1988): 120-39, provides an insightful look at the relationship between wine and aesthetic experience. Taylor argues that the contemplation of an excellent wine fosters "the free play of the imagination and the understanding. The mental powers are here free from their normal cognitive and practical functions and in this freedom mutually excite each other" (138). In her *Wine and Conversation* (Bloomington: Indiana University Press, 1983), Adrienne Lehrer provides a sophisticated linguistic analysis of the language unique to wine drinkers. Lehrer's study, by showing how "wine talk" generates its own unique lexical structure, possibly opens the door for further studies of the way in which wine drinking generates its own communal relationships and shared meanings. Another possible approach to this connection of wine drinking with Americans' unchurched aesthetic and spiritual pursuits would be to consider the anthropological literature that investigates the deeper cultural significance of food consumption patterns. For example, Claude Levi-Strauss and Margaret Mead both studied the connections between ritual food use and deeper cultural patterns or structures. Claude Levi-Strauss, *The Origin of Table Manners* (New York: Harper and Row, 1979), was particularly instrumental in opening up the use of structural analysis to examine the ways in which dietary laws and practices relate to a culture's mental and symbolic structures. A good beginning point for any anthropological study of food and wine use would be Mary Douglas, ed., *Food in the Social Order* (New York: Russell Sage Foundation, 1984), especially her introductory essay, "Standard Social Uses of Food," and William K. Powers and Marla M. Powers, "Metaphysical Aspects of an Ogala Food System." Of particular interest is the special thematic issue of the *Journal of the American Academy of Religion* 63 (Fall 1995), which contains seven articles focusing on various issues pertaining to the relationship between religion and food.

Index